If you are embarking on a journey of personal and spiritual development, what better path than the one that Jane Bain maps out in *LifeWorks*? Jane weaves together strands from both East and West, ancient and modern, mainstream and alternative – from the Sufi-like approach of teaching-tales, to the psychological theories of Carl Jung.

Stories, myths, legends and folk-tales appeal to us all on a very deep subconscious level. We identify with the characters and become immersed in the plot, wondering at the outcomes and only subconsciously aware of the multiple levels of meaning. People often become stuck in their own story, trapped in the role they have cast themself – victim, rebel, servant – without realising they can at any moment change the script of their life and turn a disaster movie into a success story.

Jane's work has been compared to that of Joseph Campbell and Julia Cameron. *LifeWorks* also draws on modern psychology, mythology, archetype, spiritualism, narrative, metaphor and complementary approaches to create a wonderful and accessible way forward.

Bridget Finklaire, Consultant Therapist & Hypnotherapist, DHypPsych, ACAHC, Registered APHP (Acc), GHR (Reg)

There's no substitute for the 'characters' that surround you and shape your everyday life. This is a wonderfully written book. The author's educational experiences shine through in this inspirational work. What attracted me most to the piece is how easy it was to read. It flowed naturally, more like a story than a self-help book. Simple examples – like the game of 'Consequences' described in the Introduction – provide anchors for the reader to grasp the philosophical discussions that follow, providing valuable insight into how a reader might improve his or her own life. This is a masterful book. Congratulations.

Richard Bard, Author (*Brainrush*)

WHAT PEOPLE ARE SAYING ABOUT

LIFEWORKS

An important and potentially life changing book. Jane Bain combines Jungian psychology with our rich mythical heritage to help us understand ourselves and transform the way we live our lives. Thoughtful and inspiring.

Helen Batten, Psychotherapist, MA (Cantab), PGDip Counselling & Psychotherapy, MBACP

This has 'bestseller' written all over it. It ranks alongside Julia Cameron's work in terms of accessibility and user-friendliness. I have been looking for a book like this for ages!

Frank McGrath, Writer and Journalist

I NEED THIS!!! I am a lecturer in film/scriptwriting/media and I need a clear, beautifully written text like this for my students. The best I've got is Chris Vogler's book *'The Writer's Journey'*. But this is even more succinct and the fact that you have taken these established archetypes and appropriated them to our lifestyles is just genius... Truly fascinating.

Carl Ashmore, Author (*The Time Hunters*) and Lecturer

I've always been fascinated by the myths and folk tales that underlie our culture and colour so much of our literature. In *LifeWorks*, Jane Bain not only clarifies the ways in which these narratives and archetypes influence our perception of the world and each other; she also suggests practical ways of using them to become more who we want to be.

If that's your goal – to live more effectively – this excellent book can add a powerful device to your toolbox.

Wendy Bertsch, Author (*Once More... From The Beginning*) and founder of website Past Times Books

A book of enormous value, both for its practical approach and its deep-rooted understanding of the role myth and archetype play in all our lives. Whether you are an author in search of inspiration for building characters, a counsellor seeking a deeper approach or an individual looking for greater understanding as well as sources of happiness in your life, this book can be life changing. In *LifeWorks*, the groundbreaking answers which enable your life to move forward are waiting for you.

Dr Charlotte Suthrell, Writer and Anthropologist

Insightful and inspirational. In the tradition of Joseph Campbell, *LifeWorks* makes myth accessible to everyone. A life-enhancing book.

Lucy Bailey, Ph.D. Sociologist

A wonderfully refreshing analysis of the archetypes that exist within us all. Jane Bain invites the reader to experience just how these archetypal characters inform and influence our lives - and discover the gift each one of them brings us. A great guide for those interested in understanding our deeper psychological and spiritual nature.

John Kent, Voice Dialogue Facilitator and Trainer

Psychologist Stanley Krippner states that "myths are narratives or statements that address existential human concerns in ways that have behavioural consequences". They serve as aids in problem-solving, interpretation and the guidance of behaviour in the resolution of human affairs, whether on a collective or personal level. *LifeWorks* presents myth as it applies to one's personal life story. I heartily recommend this book to anyone interested in becoming aware of and improving the quality of their life.

Allan Cooperstein, Ph.D. Clinical Psychologist

LifeWorks

Using myth and archetype
to develop your life story

LifeWorks

Using myth and archetype
to develop your life story

Jane Bailey Bain

BOOKS

Winchester, UK
Washington, USA

First published by O-Books, 2012
O-Books is an imprint of John Hunt Publishing Ltd., Laurel House, Station Approach,
Alresford, Hants, SO24 9JH, UK
office1@o-books.net
www.o-books.com

For distributor details and how to order please visit the 'Ordering' section on our website.

Text copyright: Jane Bailey Bain 2011

ISBN: 978 1 78099 038 5

A CIP catalogue record for this book is available from the British Library.

Design: Stuart Davies

Printed and bound by CPI Group (UK) Ltd, Croydon, CR0 4YY
Printed in the USA by Offset Paperback Mfrs, Inc

We operate a distinctive and ethical publishing philosophy in all
areas of our business, from our global network of authors to
production and worldwide distribution.

Contents

Introduction

Who am I? Why am I here? Where am I going?
What should I do now?

Ever since the first people sat around a camp fire, we have wondered about the meaning of life. One of the ways we try to answer these questions is to tell stories about ourselves. When we tell a story, we make connections between a sequence of events. By understanding how one thing led to another, we feel strengthened and reassured. We can see why things turned out this way; we can even decide what will happen next.

We make sense of the world through stories. We learn about what has happened and about what could happen. We make models of how we might behave. Stories are important, because they literally create reality. The stories we tell about ourselves affect how others see us. The stories we tell to ourselves create our sense of identity.

We look at the world around us to provide plots and role models. Sometimes the roles we see are confusing or unobtainable. Should I be a supermodel? Or perhaps a football star? If our choices are unrealistic, we are destined to disappointment. Sometimes the images are ambivalent and disturbing. Teenage wizards? Sexy vampires? These composite figures have a powerful appeal. At first sight, they seem to show exciting new possibilities. Each generation wants to make its original mark upon the world. But when we look more closely, the characters and their adventures are surprisingly familiar. The old stories still appear in modern books and films: Cinderella, Jack Giantkiller, Beauty and the Beast. The hero will save the day; the stepmother may be a witch (though possibly a white one); the wise mentor can help you on your way.

Some of the oldest stories in the world are the ones we call 'myths'. They tell of gods and heroes, great deeds and mighty monsters. Despite their supernatural setting, these stories still resonate with us today. This is because they convey deep psychological truths and spiritual insights which are relevant to the modern world. Myths contain characters whom we easily recognize: the princess, the good mother, the wise old man. The same characters re-appear in stories from different times and places. They are based on archetypes: outline figures arising spontaneously in our minds which we use to categorize and understand the people we meet.

The most important story in your life is your own story. You construct a personal narrative which helps you to make sense of the world. This 'life script' both reflects your experiences and influences your perceptions. It is based on stories you have read or heard. You allocate the parts in your story to people around you. Their roles are based on archetypal figures.

Since you were a child, you have been working on your life script. You have observed people and events in the world around you. You have unconsciously drawn on classic themes and universal figures to compose your unique personal story. You base your life script on stories you have heard, and act it out with the people around you. Some times you feel that your life is on track; at others it seems to be completely out of control. In fact, you have far more influence over your script than you realize. You can largely choose the events and characters that feature in your life. Once you are aware of this process, you can start to modify your personal story.

LifeWorks shows you how to identify relationship patterns and life themes. It is a practical handbook combining insights from psychology and anthropology. Theory, stories and exercises help you to develop your 'personal mythology'. These tools can also be used by professional counsellors, and by novelists for plot analysis and character development.

Part I: Myth and Meaning looks at why stories are important to us. It introduces the work of CG Jung and explains the concept of archetypes. You use mythic themes and common characters to compose your own life script.

Part II: Encountering Archetypes presents the twelve major archetypal figures. Each one is illustrated by a story, drawing on myths and legends from around the world. The stories are followed by points to consider and practical tasks. This work can be done on your own, or in a discussion group like a book club.

Part III: Personal Mythology helps you to identify key elements in your life script. Through a series of exercises you will learn to recognize people who conform to archetypal figures; analyze the dominant themes in your own story; and start to direct your life script.

Part I

Myth and Meaning

There is a children's party game called 'Consequences'. The players sit in a circle, each holding a pencil and a piece of paper. Each player writes a male name at the top of their sheet; folds the paper over to hide this name; and passes it to the person on their left. Next, a female name is written: the paper is folded and passed on once more. Subsequent contributors write what 'he said to her', then 'she said to him', and the final denouement. At the end, each player unfolds a paper and reads out the resulting story. Because no-one knows what the person before them wrote, the stories are quite random and often very funny.

This process is similar to the way that many people construct their lives, using stereotypes of famous personalities and fragments of story-line from books and films. We create an individual narrative drawn from our knowledge and experience of the world. This personal script is based on the possibilities which we perceive, and acted out in collaboration with the people around us. We are each the author of our own life drama, and play the principal part.

Sacred Stories

Your life is a story. You are the author of your life script and the main protagonist. Your experiences are a product of this script, and your encounters influence the next instalment. The story of your life explains who you are. Sometimes it may feel like a dramatic novel; at others, like a series of disconnected incidents. The unifying feature of your script is the central character: yourself. Whether you are conscious of it or not, you are constantly composing and revising this inner story-plan. Life choices are determined by a combination of external events and personal characteristics, but the way you decide to act depends upon your script.

We tell stories to explain things to ourselves, and to tell others about ourselves. We listen to stories because they let us learn from events that we have not experienced personally. The tales that we encounter help us to make sense of the world. Stories enable us to feel that there is some sense of purpose in life. They help us to interpret the past, to understand the present and to predict the future. Narrative is an attempt to perceive patterns in the chaos of existence. Stories imbue our lives with meaning. They give a shape to our experience and determine how we will act on subsequent occasions. Our stories affect how others see us and how we interpret our place in the world. In a very real sense, we are the stories that we tell.

From earliest times, people have told stories to make sense of their lives. These tales drew upon their experiences and elaborated on them. They allowed people to communicate information and also to try and understand the world. As people began to live in larger social groups, storytelling became more formalized. The most popular stories coalesced into cycles in which the same characters reappeared. Over time, these characters developed into pantheons of gods and heroes who personified the knowledge and values of their culture. Some of these stories were passed down as folk-tale and legend. Others were seen as having a greater social significance: these were incorporated into religious belief and ritual. The records of the deeds of these deities acquired a spiritual dimension which reflected their importance to that society. We commonly refer to these sacred stories of other cultures as 'myths'.

Myths are a way of exploring the meaning of life. They are concerned with issues that in Western society we call philosophy or religion. They address profound questions about the purpose of our existence and the factors underlying our phenomenal world.

Often the explanations they provide appear deceptively literal. With our modern sophistication we are tempted to dismiss them as stories for children. This is to profoundly misunderstand the nature of mythic thought. Whilst the stories might seem simple, they do not claim to give straightforward answers. Rather, they offer an explanation which helps us to discover an inner meaning for ourselves. Myths do not merely convey factual information, but guide us to see deeper psychological and spiritual truths.

In modern times, the word 'myth' has taken on the connotation of something untrue. To call something a myth is to imply that it is mistaken or intentionally wrong. The dictionary definition of myth includes the word 'fictitious': for example, an 'urban myth' is an apocryphal story which never actually happened. By implication, the ancient cultures whose stories we call myths are manifestly mistaken in their understanding of the world. This view fails to recognize the real significance of mythic thinking for the human psyche. To categorize traditional stories in terms of their factual accuracy is to misunderstand the real nature of mythic imagination. Myths are the Cinderella of contemporary thought, commonly overlooked and yet vital for understanding the human condition.

Why Myths Matter

Stories permeate the way we think. Whether we are aware of it or not, narrative elements form the basic structure of human thought. As individuals, families and cultural groups, we create stories to explain our place in the world and the purpose of our existence. These stories can be described as our personal myths. They may be open to conscious analysis, or taken as unquestionable basic facts about life. Often we are entirely unaware of their existence and so never question their literal truth. It is difficult to perceive the influence of family on our beliefs: when the underlying constructs of society are under consideration, it is even harder to question their objectivity.

People tell stories because they reflect important elements in the human psyche. They are public manifestations of the workings of the mind, in the same way that dreams are unconscious individual attempts to interpret reality. As human beings we are innately programmed to perceive meaning in events. Out of the deluge of sights and sounds which assault our eyes and ears, we pay selective attention to those which form a structured sequence conveying information about the world. We can listen to one person speaking in a crowded room; we read sentences on a printed page; we see faces in the drifting clouds. In the same way, people seek to perceive patterns in metaphysical events and interpret them as meaningful. We each form a model of the external world which helps us to operate effectively within it.

Myths represent the first attempts by mankind to create common meaning and impose a logical cognitive sequence upon the environment. In this sense, they are the most basic element of human culture. Myths guide the maturation of the individual psyche in line with the social needs, expectations and circumstances of the community. They draw on a body of assumptions and beliefs which underlie our perception of reality. They speak to us both as individual human beings, and as members of the wider social group. The sacred stories which we now call myths survived and evolved because they fulfilled important functions. They provided an explanation for natural events. They gave reasons which could reconcile people with their lot. Finally, they proffered spiritual sustenance in the form of a clearly defined system of belief. People turned to myth in order to understand the uncontrollable aspects of life: natural disasters, sickness, old age and death. For primitive man, myths allowed the development of a cosmology or intelligible view of the world. Myth is both the manifesto of primitive belief and a practical tool for psychic integration.

With the emergence of modern science, many people living in Western societies were alienated from this source of traditional wisdom. For the Victorians, myths were a form of primitive reasoning superseded by scientific discoveries. The gods and their adventures were clearly allegories of natural phenomena or metaphors for meteorological events. Usually the descriptions were literal, because the savage mind was obviously not equipped to deal with abstract philosophical thought. Primitive religion was contrasted to applied science, or technology, as a way of influencing events: fertilizers and pesticides are more effective than chants and invocations in assisting the growth of crops. The development of science therefore rendered mythical thought outdated and redundant. Tales of the Greek gods were relegated to the nursery bookshelf. 'Classics' became the study of Roman military strategy.

The view that myths are technologically obsolete has one major problem: it fails to account for their survival in modern times. Nineteenth-century studies of myth assumed they were concerned solely with the external world. Some myths do try to explain features of the physical environment, or provide an account of creation. If taken as a literal description of natural events, these stories appear simplistic or even absurd. Other elements, however, are sophisticated metaphors designed to promote deeper thought. More recent theories of myth have focussed on the way in which they address social issues and concerns. The stories may have an explanatory function but they also contribute to the construction of contemporary reality. Myths are set in a cultural context and address the specific concerns of the people who compose them. They influence the art and science produced by members of a given society. Mythic narratives and images structure the ways in which we see the world and largely determine our responses to it. In addition, sacred stories have a profound spiritual dimension. In the twentieth century attention shifted to the ways in which myths enable each of us to come to terms with ourselves and our place in the cosmos. Stories can help us to achieve deeper psychological understanding. This perspective is actually closer to the view of myth held in ancient times. The monster may represent an undesirable aspect of ourselves: only by confronting and overcoming our faults can we achieve personal integration. This basic human truth was widely recognized in traditional healing and shamanistic practices. The psychoanalyst Sigmund Freud proposed that in addition to its surface meaning, a myth might reveal something hidden in our unconscious minds. In his most famous example, the story of Oedipus reflects the wish of every boy for his mother's undivided attention. Freud's major insight was to recognize the influence of suppressed desires and emotions as manifest in myths and dreams. Dream symbols often refer to events which occurred in our early childhoods, perhaps no longer consciously recalled; myths contain comparable references to communal events which occurred early in the history of a people. Freud's ideas were revolutionary in his day: the fact that they now seem obvious shows the widespread acceptance they have achieved.

Myths often embody traditional values and feature super-natural protagonists and events. They take place long ago and far away, and their characters face a world very different from our own. Traditional stories can sometimes appear irrelevant to our modern lives. When myths cease to correspond to actual experience, they may start to seem invalid. They represent an alternative, and perhaps no longer relevant, mode of consciousness. To counteract this we must study myths within their social and cultural context. Stories from other times and places may reflect differences in psychological traits and moral codes. Myths from the Viking age reflect the high value placed on personal qualities such as bravery and loyalty; folktales from Africa reflect the importance of cunning and self-reliance to ensure survival. Historical and economic circumstances affect the significance of narrative events. By understanding the context in which a story was first told, we can appreciate the implicit motives and values which it conveys.

Myths still have much to teach us in the modern world. When we hear of the trials and tribulations of the heroes, we identify with them. This vicarious experience helps us adapt to the harsher realities of existence. The adventures and adversities which they encounter reflect an inner or spiritual journey. Initiation rites are a more direct form of participation: these literally transform the candidates into different people. Myths are far from being merely simple stories told to children. They are a tool for profound personal development and spiritual transformation. The surface form of the narrative encapsulates deep psychological truths. Myths help us work towards psychic integration and spiritual balance.

Human beings are the only creatures who tell stories. Other creatures use communication for amusement and instruction. Young animals play together; adults teach their offspring survival skills and inform each other about changes in the immediate environment. Animals communicate in sound-bites of experience: the honeybee's waggle; the dog's barked warning; the dolphin's cooperative calls. However, animals do not appear to analyze the world at a deeper level of meaning or under- standing. The need to formulate a rationale or identify a purpose in life is a uniquely human preoccupation. Only homo sapiens concerns himself with his place in the wider cosmos; only humans tell stories to make sense of their lives. It is no exagger- ation to say that this is the defining feature of our species. We all tell myths because we can and because we must. It is making myths that makes us fully human.

Myths may take many forms and undertake different functions, but they have one unifying definition. Myths are symbolic stories that speak to the soul.

Appendix A: The Role of Myth explains the significance of sacred stories.

Archetypal Figures

We tell stories to make sense of our world. We populate those stories with colourful characters. In describing these characters we often draw on a cast of stereotypical figures. Stereotypes provide a convenient narrative shorthand. By implying a set of attributes, we avoid the need for detailed description. We do not have to ascribe motive nor analyze actions: the people in our story are simply behaving 'in character'. These figures are usually familiar and reassuringly predictable. When someone claims to be a hero, we want him to act heroically. When someone looks like a tramp, we expect him to behave accordingly. Our images are based both on social stereotype and personal experience. The tendency to typecast seems to be an innate pattern in the human mind. Many of the same characters re-appear in stories from very different times and places. These widely recurring prototypical figures are called 'archetypes'.[1]

The concept of archetypes was first developed by the psycho-analyst Carl Jung. Archetypes are prototypical figures which arise spontaneously in the human psyche. Their outline forms consist of constellations of attributes; we fill in their features using material gathered from personal experience. These details are drawn from the people around us and developed in line with prevailing cultural values. Our image of a good mother is coloured by our own mother's behaviour; our distrust of the vagrant reflects the prejudices of our social group. The archetypal forms provide us with stock characters which we use to interpret the world. These stereotypical figures are based on common clusters of characteristics: we elaborate their features so that they take on an individual appearance for each of us. The archetypal figures in our minds are 'real' in so far as they draw on our personal experiences. They are simultaneously universal in that they are based on images from a common set of human characters.

The archetypes manifest innately and cross-culturally: the mind of a new-born child already contains outline forms which will develop into their personal pantheon. These primal figures must therefore originate in the collective unconscious. They derive from universal features of the human psyche, and so are common to all mankind. Archetypes are not directly accessible to our conscious thoughts. Rather, they are primordial images which only manifest through our interactions with the world or emerge as symbols in dreams. They also appear in stories from around the world, although their appearance is modified according to local tradition.[2]

Dreams combine images from individual memory with material from the unconscious mind. Dream symbols thus have a powerful personal psychic energy. Archetypal figures also feature prominently in myths and traditional stories. Myths present a series of images linked by a sequential narrative. They speak a symbolic language whose richness lies beyond personal experience or intellectual formulation. In the process of composing and transmitting a story, some degree of transformation and conscious elaboration must occur. For this reason we do not perceive the archetypes so clearly in stories as in dreams. Religions use stories and symbolism to communicate with their congregation. Jung suggested that the main function of religion was to provide people with myths that gave meaning to their lives. The original aim of both philosophy and preaching, namely the attainment of spiritual maturity, is now the province and goal of psychotherapy.[3]

Archetypes have a profound influence upon both our own behaviour and our perceptions of others. We use stock characters in stories and project them onto the people around us. The power of archetypes is evident in both our private and public lives. Within the family we settle into relationships based on complementary archetypal roles. These positions are comfortably familiar, and we play our parts to the best of our abilities. When we meet someone new who conforms to an archetypal figure, our attitude towards them is coloured by our image. The unconscious associations of a particular role for us may be either positive or negative: as a result we may behave either well or badly towards those around us. The way we treat others elicits self-confirming behaviour in line with our expectations: our attitude towards them is thus justified. Our prejudices provoke responses which influence our experience of the world. By becoming aware of the archetypes, we reduce our innate tendency to project them onto others. We can recognize and integrate both the positive and negative aspects of these images in our own lives. Only when we become aware of our archetypal prototypes can we see others as they really are.

Archetypal figures fall into two main groups: masculine and feminine. All of the archetypes are potentially present within everyone: the manifesting gender of an archetype simply reflects the characteristics of its fundamental energy. Jung referred to the masculine and feminine components of our nature as the animus and anima. These elements co-exist within each of us; they are complementary and compensatory. We need both types of energy to function effectively in a variety of situations. Our animus and anima direct our behaviour at different times according to our circumstances. Once we are familiar with the archetypes, we can draw on all their powers to strengthen and protect ourselves.

Female archetypes fall into three groups which reflect youth, maturity and old age. These figures have been linked since ancient times to the phases of the moon. Feminine qualities are associated with concepts of continuity and renewal: the moon may wax and wane, but each month she returns anew. The phases of a woman's life are similarly cyclical and complementary. Where female figures are identified with the moon, male characters are connected with the sun. Masculine archetypes reflect a model of personal development based on the concept of a journey. They portray a series of life stages involving the cumulative acquisition of wealth or experience. The male trajectory is one-directional: the past cannot be re-visited or revised. The hero may succeed in his quest, but he can never walk along the same path twice.

The Moon Goddess

Moon worship is the oldest form of religious practice. Prehistoric drawings record the moon's passage through the night sky. She grows from a slim crescent to a luminous orb; then, unaccountably, she starts to fade and her light diminishes until she finally disappears. For three nights the moon is dead and the night skies are dark: but then she rises again as the 'new moon'. In this recurring cycle death is not the end but signals a new beginning. The moon's progress was taken as a metaphor for human life. Like the moon, people grow to the height of their powers but then diminish and die. If the moon could return from darkness, that gave hope for mankind too.

Women are often linked with the moon, whose force dictates their monthly flow. The moon waxes and wanes, returning always to her original form. A woman may also swell with child, then resume her former shape. The phases of the moon were associated with successive stages of a woman's life. The crescent moon was personified as a young girl; the full moon as a mature woman; and the waning moon as a wise crone. These figures were seen as different manifestations of a single being, a tri-part lunar deity. When we see the sickle moon, it has a shadowy counterpart: together they make a complete orb. In the same way, each expression of the triple goddess has its darker aspect.

The moon was venerated from ancient times as the Great Mother, the source of all creative life. Models of female figures from over twenty thousand years ago feature an egg-shaped body and pendulous breasts, emphasizing her reproductive function. Such exaggerated feminine characteristics reflect the importance of fertility in subsistence societies. These models are sometimes referred to as Venus figures, but this oversimplifies their role. The Moon Goddess is far more than a mere sex symbol: she provides all of humanity with nest, breast and finally rest.

Over time, the image of this primal deity was modified by human progress. The development of agricultural techniques meant that humanity was no longer dependant on what nature offered or withheld, but could participate in the mysterious processes of production. Now tribes did not have to follow the animals on their long seasonal trails. Instead, permanent settlements developed and people began to live in stable communities. Concepts of divine providence were elaborated in line with this new method of livelihood. The role of the Great Mother, who had sent the animals to feed people, was supplemented by the Goddess of the Harvest.[4]

The great Bronze Age cultures which developed five thousand years ago in Sumeria, Egypt and Crete were built on these beliefs. The divine feminine principle was venerated as a source of life, death and regeneration. In ancient times there was no separate image of the 'terrible' mother. The Goddess could nurture, but she could also destroy: this was her prerogative and her responsibility. The chaotic aspect of the female was revered, not feared. Production and consumption were seen, not as opposites, but as complementary parts of the cycle of creation. Mother Earth is a womb, miraculously producing the crops upon which we depend; she is also our tomb, providing the shelter of our final resting place. Both functions are a necessary part of existence: the devastation of harvest yields the seeds for new growth.

The agricultural activities of planting, growth and harvest were linked to the triple image of the Great Goddess. Planting time was personified by the maiden moon; the crops grew under the care of the great mother; and the riches of harvest represented the wisdom of the matriarch. These three manifestations paralleled the evolving role of an individual mortal woman from sweetheart through matron to grandam. As time passed, the Goddess frequently acquired a male partner. He was typically portrayed as her son, a companion who was also her ritual consort. When a male sky god was introduced, his worship was complementary to veneration of the Great Mother. His presence acknowledged the complementary role of rain and sun in raising crops.[5]

This agrarian idyll was disrupted by the arrival of warrior tribesmen from the north. Armed with iron weapons, they easily overcame the indigenous population and imposed their cultural values on them. These people were nomadic herdsmen with a patriarchal social structure. Observing that only a few male animals were needed in a large flock, they believed that women's procreative role was less important than male occupations. For people whose worth was measured in livestock, the slaughter of an animal meant the permanent loss of an asset. This perception was extended to human beings, and the old cyclical concept of existence was replaced by a fearful awareness of individual mortality. Towns were heavily fortified and built on hill-tops for defence. Myths of the separation of heaven and earth reflect this emerging consciousness of the self as separate from nature.[6]

From this individualistic perspective, death was seen not as an inevitable part of life but as something to be cheated or avoided for as long as possible. If dying meant the end of the individual, then immortality could only be achieved through glorious deeds in this lifetime. This individualistic male philosophy led to the veneration of a sky god or father god, seen as the supreme lord. The mother goddess was forgotten in the exclusive propitiation of this jealous god. He was typically identified as a solar deity, shining gloriously before his eventual demise. Mortal champions were similarly equated with the sun, ascending to defeat dark forces but ultimately destined to perish. The warrior's worth was measured in terms of his fame. Thus the cult of the hero was born.

The Hero's Way

The hero is one of the strongest archetypal figures. His adventures recur in myths from around the world. Often the offspring of a god with a mortal woman, the hero symbolizes the marriage of heaven and earthly powers. The hero is called to adventure and leaves on his quest; he undergoes trials and tribulations, eventually succeeding in overcoming a monster; he attains the prize and returns transfigured to share his good fortune. The hero's quest follows a solar trajectory. A shining figure, his path is like that of the sun: rising in the morning, he vanquishes darkness only to succumb eventually to death. Although he may have supernatural strength, he is not assured a place in the afterworld: rather, it is his deeds in this life which must win him immortality. A hero is required to be brave rather than clever. Because he fights the evils which threaten society, his often amoral behaviour is conventionally forgiven. However, the hero is also required to gain a degree of self-knowledge in the course of his quest.

The hero is lauded for engaging in risk-taking behaviour because this contributes to the safety of society. His acts of bravery are honoured with public recognition and reward. In fact the real challenge is not the end but the beginning of his journey. It is at this point that he must make a commitment: and on this decision, all future possibilities depend. The chance to be a hero is not conferred but actively chosen. The boy must leave home even though he does not know where the road may take him. Prototypical heroes set off to fight monsters with a show of bravado. In real life the protagonist is sometimes reluctant; at others he is jettisoned into circumstances beyond his control. What matters is his response to this frightening state of affairs. Heroism in the true sense involves, not accomplishing the superhuman, but testing yourself to your own limits. A hero's greatest victory is that which he gains over himself.[7]

The hero's path is the universal journey which we must each undertake, although fortunately the dragons come in different sizes: you tend to get the adventure for which you are prepared. Life is a voyage in search of wisdom, often represented by a fantastical treasure or 'holy grail'. The hero plumbs the depths of the abyss and returns to the ordinary world transformed. In psychological terms, this can be interpreted as surrendering to the wisdom of the unconscious and reaping the riches thereof. The inner or spiritual journey is as important as the dramatic outward quest.

Because his story reflects universal human experience, the hero is the most easily recognized of the archetypes. The heroic ideal is manifest in everyday life. The hero is Everyman and the challenges overcome are often metaphorical monsters. The greatest heroes and heroines may be those leading the most apparently humdrum lives. Nowadays it can be hard for young people to identify their heroic task. Traditional initiation rituals transformed a boy into a man, often leaving physical scars to indicate his altered status. Responsibilities of work and family reinforced the importance of his new role. In the modern world we lack the rites of passage which would once have guided us. By postponing adulthood, we are not so much indulging young people as depriving them of meaning in their lives.[8]

The heroic ideal has been extremely influential on popular culture. Artists, novelists and songwriters have paid tribute to it; films such as the Star Wars trilogy exemplify the classic cyclical model of the hero's quest. However, the heroic task is only part of a greater journey. The cult of the champion is properly complemented by honouring the wisdom of the sage. The prince grows up to be a king, but eventually he will become old in turn. The male archetypes in the following stories portray the lighter and darker aspects of these stages of life.

Life Scripts

We tell stories to understand what has happened to us. We also use them to tell people about ourselves. When we tell stories about ourselves, we construct a social character. When we compose these stories in our minds, we form a sense of self. Each of us has a unique story to relate. We choose what to include in this story, and decide what to leave out. We integrate the events in our lives into a meaningful narrative. This structured composition is both descriptive and predictive. How we interpret our past experience affects our current responses and future plans. Our personal history shapes our expectations about what is likely to happen next. The story that we like to tell about ourselves can be called our 'life script'. It includes both an apparently objective description of things that have happened to us and a subjective interpretation of our personal relationships. Your script determines both your actions and reactions in new situations, ensuring that your life story will have consistency.[9]

Our story is based both on what has happened to us and on how we view those events. These two factors interact in complex ways to produce our individual life histories. Some things are obviously outside our control. The social and economic conditions into which we were born will have a profound influence on our early experience. Major natural disasters may plunge us into circumstances which we had no way of planning for. However, the way we interpret events is more important than external factors in determining what we will experience next. This is because our responses tend to draw us into situations in line with our expectations. The way we habitually behave ensures that our future experiences will probably be similar to our past ones.[10]

We actually have more control over our life stories than we sometimes think. We each compose a 'plan for living' which contains both dramatic narrative and character parts. We select our life themes from stories we have come across in both fiction and real life. The sources for our stories are the world around us: books, films, newspapers, parental proselytising and social example are all potential sources of influence. The narrative plots which we choose are those which resonate most deeply with us. We need real actors to play the parts in our story; we allocate these roles to the people around us. Their actual behaviour towards us will be influenced by both the demands of our story and our expectations of them based on their resemblance to archetypal figures.

Part II

Encountering Archetypes

You take the first step, and the story starts:
Picking a path among the branching ways
You chart a course, a new untraveled road
Hoping to find new meaning for your days.
You choose one way, and you can never know
Towards what place the other path would go.

But everywhere you go, you seem to find
Familiar faces staring back at you.
You hurry on, but soon you start to see
That these are people whom you always knew.
Hard as you run, you cannot leave behind
The archetypal figures in your mind.

So greet them; let them join you on the way
Since they will always follow where you go
Be welcoming and talk to them as friends
To learn why they have manifested so.
Omega comes from alpha, end from start:
Your destiny is written by your heart.

In this section you will meet the twelve major archetypal figures. You will learn their main features and meet examples from literature, film and public life. For each figure you can read a story, based on myth or legend. After every story you will find questions to consider and a task to complete. If you do the exercises you will engage more fully with the story. You will find it easier to recognize this figure as it manifests in your own life, and be able to draw on the power of the archetype when it can help you. The work can be done on your own and at your own pace. Alternatively the stories can form the basis for a regular discussion group, along the lines of a book club. It would be helpful to have a notebook where you can keep a record of your thoughts and jot down any examples of the archetypes that you encounter.

You will soon discover that the work that you do here is only the beginning. Once you have become familiar with the archetypes, you will find that you meet them everywhere. Novelists and scriptwriters use them in their work: from the depths of Dostoevsky to TV shows like *Dallas*, these figures are the basis for characters in books, plays and films. Archetypal projections form the basis for hero-worship and witch-hunts by the media. They account for the roles adopted by politicians, as they oscillate between playing the hero and the wise old man. They explain the ways in which we interact with people in our own lives. We project personalities and motives onto others in accordance with our unconscious archetypal templates. At the same time, we unconsciously adopt complementary roles which reinforce our perceptions. By learning to recognize the archetypes, you will be able to deal with them when you encounter them.

The archetypal figures have been divided into male and female groups. This categorization reflects the masculine and feminine energies of the psyche. Male characters tend to engage in action and analysis. Feminine characters are typically concerned with empathy and emotion. Each group contains three types of figure: young, adult and old. The three manifestations of the feminine principle each have their masculine counterparts. The figures within each category are presented in complementary pairs. Thus, the three stages of childhood, adulthood and old age each have their brighter and darker aspects. The darker beings represent the alter egos of the lighter: they are complementary and not necessarily negative. The lighter figures focus on helping others and the communal good; the darker beings are more concerned with self-development. Each archetype has many manifestations, but all are aspects of these twelve major prototypes.

When we encounter people in real life, their characters are not so clear cut. Archetypes present a set of attributes, sometimes tending towards a stereotype. Not all of the archetypal features will be applicable to a real person. If we judge someone on the basis of a single characteristic, such as religion or nationality, we are guilty of prejudice. Similarly we must be careful not to ascribe character traits to someone on the basis of our subconscious projections. Once we are aware of our tendency to perceive people in terms of prototypes, we can modify our automatic assumptions with evidence based on our own observations.

Just as we must take care not to project archetypal characteristics, we should be wary of over-identifying with a particular archetype ourselves. We each contain aspects of every archetype, whether or not we consciously identify with it: all their features potentially reside within ourselves. It is important to acknowledge these complementary characteristics rather than rejecting them. Like the reformed smoker or the homophobic male, we often criticize other people for doing things we would like to try ourselves. Sometimes we need to be able to draw on the darker aspects of our personality. A man in a 'tricky' position may resort to cunning and subterfuge. A woman disciplining her children may have to use 'tough love'. We can also draw on the power of archetypes from the opposite gender. A man may 'mother' a friend or partner in emotional distress; a woman may act as a 'hero' in defence of someone or something she loves.[1]

Archetypal figures always interact with their necessary counterparts. The great mother needs a child to nurture; the hero needs an ogre to fight or a princess to protect. Whilst each of these stories focuses on a main protagonist, characters with features of other archetypes inevitably appear. These figures interact with the central subject, and their encounters tell us more about him. This reflects the way in which we relate to those around us in conformity with our archetypal expectations. It is precisely because they resonate so deeply with our own experience that the stories are so enthralling.

By their nature, the same archetypal figures recur in every tradition of storytelling. Whether the stories have a sacred or secular purpose, the characters in them are similar. It is because they resonate with something deep in our minds that these tales are so effective and enduring. Using archetypal images is a powerful narrative technique. The priests of old knew it when they encoded esoteric religious truths in simple story form. Modern novelists use it when they present ancient themes in the guise of contemporary dilemmas. We experience it directly when we are moved by a book or play or film. We recognize and respond to these figures because they are indelibly etched in the human psyche. As such, we unconsciously incorporate them into our own life stories.

The clearest examples of the archetypes occur in traditional tales which have been refined over many generations. The stories which have been chosen to illustrate them here are drawn from many different times and countries. Some of them might be classified as myth, others as legend or folk-tale. The categorization is spurious if we view all these stories as lying on a continuum. Myths tell of a time before history began and relate the exploits of gods and supernatural beings. Legends occur on the cusp of myth and history; they tell of the achievements of mortal heroes. Folk-tales take place in the timeless here-and-now and are concerned with the activities of Everyman. Myths were originally the preserve of a priestly hierarchy and legends were used by early historians. By contrast, folk-tales were stories typically related by women to an audience of children. They constitute a legacy of social wisdom which is passed from the older to the younger generation. Because of this, folk-tales often provide particularly clear examples of archetypal characters.

Table 1: Archetypal Figures

	Young	Mature	Old
Female			
Light	Princess	Good Mother	Grandmother
Dark	Clever Girl	Wild Woman	Wicked Witch
Male			
Light	Infant Prince	Hero	Wise Man
Dark	Urchin	Trickster	Ogre

Female Archetypes: The Triple Muse

Women's lives are cyclical, reflecting their relationship with the moon. Each individual woman grows from girlhood to maturity, and finally to old age; but within this trajectory their bodies are subject to the fluctuations of the monthly cycle. Whilst a man may maintain a constant physical form, women swell and subside under the influence of mysterious natural forces. Women's bodily transformations are paralleled by changes in role and psyche. Feminine concern with appearances is often not vanity, but a concern to exalt or veil these inner processes.

Women's wisdom concerns collaboration with these natural forces. It is women who control the interface between nature and culture. Women transform raw food into cooked meals, weave natural fibres into warm clothes, and turn mewling infants into functional human beings. As mothers and teachers, they preserve and transmit the basic elements of human society. In this nurturing role the female is responsible for more than just her personal wellbeing. Whereas the male hero faces a simple choice – vanquish or perish – the heroine in concerned with the survival of herself and her dependants. To this end she will use whatever comes to hand, transforming it as the moment demands. Spinning is a metaphor for transformation, and spinning is women's work. When a woman makes a home she is truly spinning straw into gold.

As they move through life, women must take on different roles and responsibilities. To meet these needs they must themselves transform. Since they are physically weaker than men, women must be spiritually strong to survive. They are flexible and yielding, making the necessary adaptations to whatever situation they find themselves in. Sleeping Beauty pricks her finger upon a spindle and falls into a deep pubescent sleep. Fleeing from the unwanted attentions of Apollo, Daphne turns into a laurel tree. Captured by Peleus, the nymph Thetis becomes a pillar of burning fire. The transformations are irrevocable and often painful, but each new role has advantages too. Myths and fairy-tales illuminate the metamorphoses necessary at each stage of life and reconcile us to these changes.

Female archetypes reflect the triple face of the Moon Goddess. They fall into the three stages of life, namely the maiden, mother and matriarch. Unlike male archetypes, they are rarely either wholly good or bad. The moon passes from light to dark, and the only predictable thing about it is that it will eventually return. Due to their inconstant nature, women may be portrayed as unreliable (from a male perspective) or flexible (from a female viewpoint). This unpredictability makes women dangerous since they threaten the male-ordained social order. The maiden is beautiful and desirable, but she is also fickle. The mother is strong and nurturing, but she can also be controlling and even destructive. The matriarch is wise, but the crone may misuse her knowledge for dark ends. Men have been inspired by women to perform great deeds of valour; they have exalted the beauty of the Muse in songs and poems; but at times their actions have been motivated by darker fears. Stories about women reflect this pervasive ambivalence concerning female power.[1]

As a tri-part deity, the goddess often appears in multiple aspects within a single story. When the heroine is a young girl she may be helped by a loving mother or wise grandmother. Conversely, she may be hurt or hindered by an evil stepmother or wicked witch. In stories where a young girl suffers, it is often at the hands of an older woman. Stories like Cinderella's occur throughout the world, bearing witness to the harm done by women to other women. The symbols of Cinders' moral superiority vary with cultural values, but her maternal deprivation and ultimate triumph are constant features. When a motif becomes so widespread, it indicates a deeper underlying meaning. In this case we can see that the main characters are inextricably linked.

An older woman may represent a future self, who inducts the young girl through a painful initiation for her own good. Only by undergoing these trials and tribulations will the heroine attain spiritual maturity.

The psyche may pay homage to factors which the conscious mind cannot acknowledge. We see this in the behaviour of every teenager trying to escape from family bonds. The adolescent is caught between love and resentment, circling the mother planet like a reluctant asteroid. It is both necessary and desirable for them to build up enough 'centrifugal force' to break free. The wicked stepmother forces the real daughter to leave her father's house: thanks to her, the persecuted girl reaches womanhood, symbolized by a home and husband of her own. By manifesting simultaneously in her multiple aspects, the Moon Goddess demonstrates the range of her powers and responsibilities. Unlike the solar male, the thrust of whose story depends upon his response to external events, the focus of the lunar female is on inner change and self-development. The great mother is thus alpha and omega, containing the beginning and the end of all our stories.

1. The Princess

Fair and pure, the princess is one of the most potently alluring archetypes. Full of the potential of youth, she represents the ideal young woman in terms of both beauty and behaviour. The princess is defined not by her crown but by her demeanour. Even when dressed in rags she always behaves with courtesy and consideration. Her status does not rest upon accumulation of material wealth, but rather upon the nobility of her nature. She epitomizes the potential of the base self to transform into higher spirit through the redeeming power of love. The colour most often associated with her is pink, the aura of the dawn. As such, she is the incarnation of hope and new beginnings.

We first meet the princess in fairy tales on our mother's knee. We can identify with the heroine of these stories because she is also young. Like us, she has little control over what happens to her. These stories actually have deeper meanings that, like their heroines, lie dormant until we are ready to receive them. Sleeping Beauty waits sedately for the turmoil of adolescence to pass. Snow White retreats to an infantile domain where she does not have to face the implications of her emerging sexuality. Rapunzel is locked up, forbidden to even leave her room. We are happy for things to stay this way, secure in our confinement, until we have finished growing up ourselves.

In general the princess is a passive figure. Pretty yet demure, she is a safe receptacle for our dreams. The ivory tower may be dull but it is at least secure. The princess is not yet able to cope with the world outside: it is safer for her to stay indoors until she has grown up. The dangers of adult life are often represented by a beast which threatens to devour the young girl. If the threat becomes too pressing, the princess may need a knight to help her. The 'damsel in distress' is a recurrent motif in legend and fairy-tale. Perseus saves Andromeda from a sea-monster; Saint

George rescues his princess from a fearsome dragon. Of course, not every princess is as helpless as this stereotype implies. We may hope for a hero even though we are perfectly capable of getting along without him. The princess may be in a difficult predicament but she might not want to be indebted to a macho male. Sometimes we suspect it is actually the hero who needs a part to play. When Richard Gere climbs up to Julia Roberts' window at the end of *Pretty Woman*, we are in no doubt about who is saving whom.[1]

We find the princess appealing as a little girl but her image is not always appropriate for an adult woman. When we encounter her later on in life, her behaviour has changed surprisingly little. Shirley Temple on celluloid sings and dances forever like a living doll. Katherine Hepburn in *The Philadelphia Story* is trapped in an unsustainable self-image. Juliet will never know the ups and downs of marriage with her Romeo. A real-life princess, Diana was lauded for her beauty and kindness but forbidden by her public to behave like an adult woman. Looking at these grown girls we can learn a salutary lesson about the dangers of never growing up. It is fine to dream about our prince, but we cannot wait for him too long. Sooner rather than later we must take responsibility for our own welfare.

The girl in most fairy stories is young, but she is not a little child. We identify with her adventures because she manifests the transition from innocence to maturity. One popular version of the princess archetype is the role of the 'runaway bride'. The girl in this story is on the threshold of womanhood, but not yet quite ready for commitment. The princess returns unsullied from her adventures: due to her noble nature she has been able to transcend the dangers encountered along the way. Her faithfulness is rewarded by the bliss of eternal love. No obstacle can keep the couple apart since it is their destiny to be together. The reunion of the loyal lovers enables renewal of the marriage vows which are the closing passage of many fairy stories. This story has many variants, in which a couple are inadvertently separated but ultimately reunited. The suitor welcomes back his bride because her essential chastity is still untouched.[2]

In the West we have all heard of beautiful Helen, reclaimed by her husband Menelaus after the ten-year siege of Troy. In India, many of the same themes occur in the *Ramayana*. The 'Journey of Rama' is one of the best-known and loved stories in the world. This epic poem relates Rama's courtship of the beautiful Sita; his unfair banishment from his father's domain; and their blissful life together in the forest. Later on, Sita is abducted by the demon Ravana and taken to Lanka, but Rama rescues her with the help of the Monkey General Hanuman. The following story, 'Song of Sita', retells the first part of this classic tale.[3]

At the start of the story, Sita is the archetypal princess. Protected and cherished, she awaits the arrival of the suitor who will claim her hand in marriage. She is outwardly passive yet inwardly turbulent, yearning for the unique adventure that fate has in store for her. The princess in each of us reflects this eternal state of expectancy. When we are young, we sense that we are innately special. To our teenage frustration, the world fails to acknowledge and honour our unique gifts. As we grow older, we learn that we have to activate our own destinies. The task of the princess is to channel her dreams into a source of life energy.

Song of Sita

(An Indian Story)

I am Sita. I sit on the ground beneath a great tree and the wind breathes on my bare arms. My hair pours around me like a waterfall. The wonderment of existence absorbs me utterly. I am transfixed in this moment of being.

Later I will go back to the house and wait for him to come home. My lips curl, remembering our first meeting. I did not dream that he would be the one. How cross I was when Mama mentioned that Aunty would be calling with another boy. We were sitting at the kitchen table and I was wearing my new jeans. It was too hot for them, really, but when my papa was out I could dress as I pleased. Just at that moment there was a tap-tap at the door. Mama had left it to the last moment in hopes of catching me off-guard. She is always worrying or scheming about something, my mama: sometimes I could give her a hard slap. She looked at me with bag-eyes and her mouth was trembling. Suddenly I felt sorry for her and scuttled obediently upstairs. I took my time changing, listening to the sound of voices from the front room. When I had left it as long as I could, I shimmied back down in my third-best sari. Aunty and the prospect were settled in the big chairs. I joined Mama sitting demurely on the settee.

After a while I slung a glance towards him. He was looking down at his hands, playing with his knuckles. I registered the visibles: slim, average height, hair carelessly combed. He probably didn't want to be going through this rigmarole any more that I did. But then he looked up and saw me watching him. His face did not move at all, but he stopped twisting his hands. His eyes went very dark, twin trapdoors opening onto endless space. My stomach dropped like a bucket in a well. I could really hear the thudding of my heart. Then the power rushed through me like a warm flood. I tipped my face down to hide the flush, but I could still sense him staring at me. We sat on opposite sides of the room but my body shook under his caress. I knew he wanted me and rejoiced in the glory of it.

The voices pattered on and now Rama was trying to make a favourable impression. He told Mama at length about the family business. He had two brothers and there were good prospects for expansion. None of them were married, but he himself was hoping to settle down soon. (This was apparently a pleasant surprise for Aunty, who audibly gasped). On the way out, Mama apologized for the broken gatepost and he offered to come back the next day and fix it. The aura of approval hovered smugly above us in the midday heat.

And so it was all arranged between the families. I would not be going back to school in the autumn. An opportunity like this was too good for me to miss. I smile again, remembering how jealous my friends were that my life was to be so smooth. I looked forwards to the freedom of being a woman at last, away from the suffocation of my papa's support and Mama's love. We talked for hours on the telephone, planning our future together. Sometimes we would meet, suitably chaperoned by friends, each rendezvous sealed with a coy kiss. Wrapped in each other's arms he would strain against me, frustrated yet respectful: I would turn my face away discreetly and exult in the force of his desire.

Fast-forward to the next key stage of my life. We are officially engaged, and my parents go to meet his family. Only now does there turn out to be a problem. The other sons are only half-brothers; his father has married again. And there is only one bedroom for the boys. Stepmother does not see why we should have it and frankly I am inclined to agree. This woman is a real bitch. The sort who wears her best clothes every day, just to remind you that she is worth it and everyone else is an inferior being. She has persuaded the father that her elder son is the brightest and should take over the day-to-day running of the business: inherit the family empire, as you might say. To this end she will even forgo the pleasure of having a daughter-in-law to order around. I think we are well out of it, but obviously this presents some practical problems.

In the end it is agreed that Rama should spend some time away at college. This makes the father feel a little better about betraying his eldest son for the sake of pillow-play. He can study accountancy. It is a respectable profession, and perhaps one day he can even come back and re-join the family firm. To do him credit, his brother has a private word and promises him equal shares in the business when he does return. Rama is most upset and wants to call off our engagement. It will be years before I am able to support you properly, he says. But I have kissed him and felt his need for me. He wants me as a man wants a girl, of course, but we are also responding to a deeper force. Our souls acknowledged each other from the day we met. We are true partners, committed for life like swans. I believe our spirits met when the world was made: our love is something special, sacred, eternal. He is the other half of myself: I could live without him but there would be no colour in my world. Besides, there is my reputation to think of. If he were seen to repudiate me now, people might start to talk. It is not good for a girl to have a string of boyfriends after her name. So we agree not to consider that as an option. In our hearts we are already committed and a wife's duty is to share her husband's lot.

So we are wedded and I come here with him. It is a campus college with married quarters. We have a little place of our own looking out across this park. The youngest brother comes too, ostensibly to help us settle in. I suspect he really just wants to get away for a while. But then their father has some small emergency, so he has to go home. Rama could hardly leave so near the start of his studies. Besides, I think he still feels a little upset about the whole affair. So each morning he gets up whilst I am still half-asleep, kisses me and picks up his bag full of books. Then he drops it and comes back to kiss me again. I put my arms around his neck and turn my face up to him. I am drunk with the joy of my love. Then the door bangs, and he is finally gone. When the sheets have cooled I get up and wash his breakfast things. Afterwards I comb my hair and go out into the park. I sit in the shade under my favourite tree. The leaves whisper secrets which I can almost hear. I watch the people going about their business. I wait to see what will happen today.

I am Sita and everything is me.

I sit within the dark cascade of my hair.

The warm wind strokes me like my lover's touch.

Any minute now, any moment, my life will truly begin.

******

Think about...

When do you think this story is set? Where does it take place? What clues tell you this? How does the setting influence the course of events?

How do you feel when you read this story? Do you identify with Sita, or think that she is too self-absorbed? Why might she feel and act as she does?

Does Sita remind you of anyone you know? How do you relate to this other person? Have you come across similar characters in books or films? What do you think of them?

Do you think Sita behaves like a princess? How should a real princess think? ...speak? ...act?

Can you think of a time when you felt like a princess?

Task

When you are young, it is easy to believe that you are somehow special. As the years go by, your self-esteem can be dimmed by the duties of daily life. Sometimes you need to feel safe and cherished. One way to do this is to have a place which is set aside exclusively for you. This space does not need to be large or luxurious: it just has to provide a haven where you can feel truly yourself.

Picture your bedroom when you were about seven years old. Imagine it in as much detail as you can: where your bed was; the colour of the curtains; the pictures on the walls; where you stored your clothes; where you kept your most precious possessions. How did you feel when you were in this room? What made this space especially yours?

Now think about your bedroom today. How do you feel when you are in it? How could you make this place more special for yourself? This could be something as radical as painting all the walls purple or as simple as buying a few candles to put on a chest of drawers. If you share a sleeping space, perhaps there is another corner of the house which you could claim as your own.

Decide what you would like to change and fix a date to do it.

2. The Clever Girl

We meet the clever girl in myths and legends from around the world. The best-loved versions of her story are the ones we call folk or fairy-tales. In the classic example, a peasant's daughter has to complete an almost impossible task. Typically the girl has not gone looking for adventure but when it arrives she rises to the occasion. Like her urchin counterpart she is poor in material goods although richly endowed in other ways. If she is of royal blood, the family has fallen on hard times. If she has siblings, the girl is the youngest child so cannot expect to receive a substantial dowry. She must make her own way in the world, relying on her quick wits and courage.

Because kindness is seen as a desirable female characteristic, the girl is usually good-hearted as well as clever. Often the story begins with the girl given a choice between receiving a small piece of bread and her mother's blessing, or a whole loaf and her mother's curse. By opting for the blessing, the girl acknowledges how much her mother has already given her and so is able to benefit from her psychological inheritance. When several sisters face the same trial it is the youngest daughter who makes the correct choice and thereby ensures her ultimate success.

Like real life, fairy-tales often feature girls who through no fault of their own are placed in adverse circumstances. The heroine survives through a combination of bravery and resourcefulness. She may dress in rags, but her outward appearance only conceals her inner worth. Beauty goes to meet her Beast in keeping with her father's promise: when she learns to love him, his own true character is correspondingly revealed. The miller's daughter is placed in a difficult position by her father's claim: she tries to deal fairly with the little man who comes to her aid, but Rumpelstiltskin's boasting betrays him. The princess whose brothers have been turned into swans weaves seven shirts from nettles to break the enchantment. Cinderella does not sit around feeling sorry for herself: her good nature gains her new friends. In many versions of her story, it is not a fairy but a tree she tends which bestows her blessings. Life may be tough at times but at no point do we doubt that there will be a happy ending. Stories of clever girls making good are especially gratifying because we feel that justice has been done. As in the real world, hard work is a good substitute for other gifts.

Clever girls frequently feature in literature, partly because clever girls can write books. The heroine is usually smart, but not conventionally beautiful: we identify with this because few of us are entirely confident of our own good looks. She wins through by dint of her personality, combined with a dose of well-deserved luck. We know from the first lines of *Gone With The Wind* that Scarlett O'Hara can take care of herself. It is important for the clever girl to find a partner whom she can respect as an equal. When Elizabeth Bennett overcomes her prejudice to recognize Darcy as her true mate, we breathe a sigh of relief. Sometimes a girl is too clever for her own good. Estella in *Great Expectations* is 'knowing', using her feminine wiles to exploit men: only at the end does she learn to respect Pip's loyalty.

Things have not always gone so smoothly for clever girls as they do in these stories. In many times and places, it has not been acceptable for a woman to be too smart. Female intellectuals have been labelled as 'bluestockings' or put down in less subtle ways. A traditional saying advises that 'A woman, a dog and a walnut tree – the harder you beat them, the better they be.' An intelligent woman is a category violation, an affront against nature. The clever girl is clearly untrustworthy: people instinctively see her as a young sorceress. Her rehabilitation through books and films about glamorous teenage witches is still tinged with a slight ambivalence about her real motives. Really clever girls do not reveal the full extent of their powers.

The following story tells of a girl who has to test her wits against extra-natural adversaries. In old times there was a widespread belief that the wilder areas of Britain were inhabited by 'little folk', a small dark race who preferred to stay hidden and were afraid of running water and cold iron. The precursors of modern fairies, these beings might help around the farm if treated correctly, but could wreak havoc if slighted. The old ones had skills and knowledge of their own, enabling them to move silently through the countryside and utilize herbal remedies. They were often referred to as the 'good folk', this being a propitiatory appellation designed to invoke their favour. They sometimes waylaid travellers with offers of hospitality: if accepted, one night's feasting might mean an absence of a year or a century of human time. The little folk sometimes took a human child to replenish their stock, replacing it with one of their own babies. A changeling child could be identified by its sickly aspect, for they would not thrive in the mortal world.[1]

The Changeling Child

(An Old English Story)

Our Molly was never much to look at, but she was a clever one. She was always asking about this or that, and putting two and two together to make five. Mother used to say that she had found the favour of the fairies. Molly would laugh and reply that she'd sooner have got wealth or beauty than brains. Still, there's no denying that she knew the ways to bring plenty and prosperity, and that's not a thing to be sneezed at.

She may not have been born in a soft bed, but she certainly made sure of her own luck. She was careful never to walk under a ladder, nor look at the new moon through a glass window. She never sat thirteenth at a table, but would jump up to serve the others. If she spilt salt she'd throw a pinch over her shoulder, and never mind the cost. We only had a brass mirror between us, so she couldn't break that in any case. She went to church regularly too, so there was none that could point a finger at her for heeding the old customs. Mother let her dress in green for it suited her, though there are some that say it's an invitation for trouble: but the good folk had always been kind to her, and Molly was respectful of their ways.

The older girls had taken their dowries and married, and there was not much left for Molly. Not that she was in a hurry to leave home, for that girl was happy wherever she might be. The only reason she went out to work was that a woman in the next village needed some help. It was not far, but that day's walk seemed a long way to young Molly. When she arrived the house was dark, and she knocked on the door with some misgivings. The farmer opened it and he looked glad enough to see her. His wife had a baby, and she was lying in bed too weak to get up and see to anything. Molly felt sorry for the couple, and she set about putting the place in order. In no time at all she got a good fire going and a pot of soup on the boil. The room was a good deal homelier that night than it had been for a long while.

She felt sorrier for them next morning when she had a good look at the baby. It was a dark scrawny little thing with its face and hands screwed up tight, and always crying. Molly suspected right off that something was wrong, but she knew that she must be careful. That first day she just cleaned the house and prepared the evening meal. She made sure the woman had enough to eat, and she took the child for a while to let her rest. The baby hushed in her arms and that made Molly even more suspicious, for it's not right when a child prefers a stranger to its own mother. When the farmer came in, Molly closed the shutters and served his supper. Outside, the wind was wuthering wildly and she felt sure that the house was being watched. At bedtime she took an oatmeal cake and left it by the hearth for the little folk, in thanks for their good will.

Next morning the chores were done before Molly got down from the loft. She was grateful, but she worried more than ever about that child. She got the meal ready, and then she went out to look around the farm. Just as she had suspected, there was a big hawthorn bush growing fast by the outhouses. Nothing wrong with that on its own, but it would certainly provide cover for the wrong sort of attentions. She looked into the barn, and found the farmer wringing the last drops from his cow. Molly went back inside and got a small bowl to fill with milk for the good folk. She left it just outside the barn door, underneath the hawthorn bush. Sure as eggs is eggs, the milk will increase if you invite the little ones to tend your livestock and share the produce with them.

On the third day, Molly went walking in the fields around the farm. She found what she was looking for and brought it back hidden under her cloak, for she did not want to alarm the household. That evening, when the farmer and his wife went to bed, she offered to tend the baby. They were glad enough at the

43

prospect of a good night's sleep. As soon as she was sure they were snoring, Molly pulled out the elderflower branch that she had cut that afternoon. She threw it on the fire and stirred the embers into a good flame. Then she flung open the shutters and called aloud:

"This one's been here long enough, and that one's been gone too long. Come and collect your own!"

And with that, she picked up the baby and dropped him into the fireplace.

There was a terrible scream, and a swirling gust of wind. The fire blazed up and all the candles went out. Molly shielded her eyes and flattened herself to the wall. She was truly afraid that this time she had gone too far. Everything went dark, and there was a fearsome scraping sound. Then she heard the noise of a child crying.

Molly opened her eyes again and looked around. The fire was out, but a faint light crept in through the windows. The changeling child was gone, but there on the hearth lay a baby crying lustily. Molly picked up the infant and wiped it with her apron. The baby hit out with its little fists and howled more loudly for its mother. The farmer's wife came rushing in, having heard the noise, and seized the child in her arms. The farmer came running after her in his nightshirt: he fair froze with the shutters wide as they were. Molly had a fair job explaining the cause of the commotion. The following day she was careful to take the ashes of the elderfire outside and throw them as far from the house as she could. She was a clever girl, and respected the ways of the good folk, and they never held that night's events against her. They always helped her with her work and she never forgot to leave out milk and oatcakes to thank them. The farmer's wife hung a cross round her baby's neck for protection, and the child thrived from that day forth. But the farmer took a long iron knife and fastened it above the doorway, lest the fairies ever be tempted to look into the house and see how their foster child was faring.

******

Think about...

Why do you think this story was first told? Was it to scare the audience, or teach them? What can we learn from this story? According to traditional wisdom, what must we do to keep ourselves safe?

Molly has a good heart and a store of practical knowledge. Where do you think some of these beliefs originated? Why might some of them be effective?

How does Molly show that she is a clever girl? Which helps more, her knowledge or her attitude? Was the risk that she took justified? What would you have done in her place?

What other characters and relationships does the story portray? Have you ever been involved in similar relationships? If so, how do you feel about the people concerned now?

Molly manages to protect those in her care. Do you have any protective rituals or lucky charms? Where do they come from? When might you use them now?

Task

Picture yourself at fifteen years old. Remember what it felt like to be you at that age. What did you look like? Where did you live? Which were your favourite songs? How did you spend your free time? Who were your best friends?

The clever girl can take care of herself. In real life, it helps to have friends whose faith gives you confidence in yourself. True friends believe in you and help you to be the person whom you want to be. Choose your companions carefully, for they midwive your life experience. Their perceptions reinforce your self-image; their expectations influence how you behave. On many levels, who you know is just as important as what you know.

Think of three friends who make you feel treasured: people who value you for being yourself. Find something that reminds you of each friend: it could be a gift from that person, an object reflecting a common interest or a picture that reminds you of a shared experience. You might decide to make something special for this purpose, such as a compilation of music that you both enjoy or a scrapbook about a holiday you took together. Invite each person round for a meal to share this and celebrate your friendship.

3. The Good Mother

Our earliest experience revolves around our mothers. Whether we remember it consciously or not, we once depended on her for everything. As infants we were completely reliant on others. Our need for affection is even greater than our need for nourishment, though food is often given as a metaphor for love. If our needs are met we grow into balanced adults who can give and receive love; but an emotionally deprived child may never fully recover. An over-abundance of affection is just as dangerous. The 'smother mother' will never release her children to live their own lives. Spoiling a child creates stifling bonds of maternal debt. Mothers are the source of all succour, but they must also introduce us to discipline. The ambivalence that many men feel about women reflects this dual nature of the maternal role.

Our image of the good mother emphasizes her nurturing and protective functions. The Great Mother is a primal deity, responsible for the creation of the world. She represents woman at the height of her productive and reproductive powers. As a goddess she is a fertility figure, responsible for the creation and procreation of mankind. She is the full moon, the central figure in the divine lunar trinity. The oldest cave paintings include emblems to invoke her protection. She is Gaia, the earth-mother, caring for the plants and animals on which people depend. When we talk of our planet as Mother Earth, we are honouring an ancient tradition.

The Great Mother is also incarnate within mortal women. She has many faces, for it is the nature of the female to be adaptable. As an adult woman the mother is responsible for the care of her social group. In Britain the Queen is the symbolic mother of the nation. In America the President's wife implicitly fills the same role. As an individual, a woman may be a parent producing children of her own. She may also be a teacher or nurse, fostering the young and caring for the elderly. Florence Nightingale was a 'good mother' to the soldiers in the Crimean War. Wendy is a 'little mother' to Peter Pan and his lost boys. Novels and biographies remind us of the mother's lasting influence. Ma in *Little House on the Prairie* and Marmee in *Little Women* are quintessential models of motherhood: refined yet resilient, they are truly 'steel magnolias'. The Great Mother is indisputably feminine, yet fierce in defence of those in her care. Her nurturing duties are a product, not of biological determinism, but of archetypal role.[1]

Far older than the god of the major monotheistic religions, the Great Mother appears in many incarnations across time and space. She is Nut, the Egyptian sky goddess, whose star-spangled body arches protectively over the world. She is invoked by the bare-breasted priestess of ancient Crete, dressed in a long flounced skirt and grasping two serpents in her raised hands. The Greek creation myth tells how Gaia emerged from Chaos and made Ouranos, the star-crowned sky, to be her partner and lie over her: she then bore a generation of deities who personify the forces of Nature. One of her grandchildren was Demeter, the goddess of fertility and agriculture, who nurtures the plants and creatures in her care.

Demeter herself is the earth mother who produces all crops and vegetation. As the Great Mother she can choose to dispense or withhold her bounty. Her very name indicates her power to meter or measure out life. Her daughter is Kore, the Grain Maiden, who is abducted by Hades, Lord of the Underworld. After her marriage Kore is known as Persephone, the awful one, which literally means that those who behold her are filled with awe. When Demeter loses her daughter she is inconsolable, bereft of the only company she desires. The ensuing barrenness of the land is an outward reflection of this spiritual desolation. When we hear Demeter's story we know the eternal longing of a woman for her child. For Demeter, motherhood is her defining role: within the apparent bonds of her responsibilities the good mother finds fulfilment.[2]

Demeter's Daughter

(A Greek Myth)

Happiness is a state of mind, they say, but for me paradise is a place and a time. I can be more specific: happiness was the hills above Eleusis before my daughter was taken from me.

We were always so close, she and I. We walked together through the meadows, delighting in each growing thing. As the warm sun caressed the crops, we talked of the harvest to come. Her hair was gold and rippled like the ripening corn. On her head she wore a circlet of summer flowers. The animals of the woods and fields came to her hand. She was the loveliest creature of them all. Kore, I called her: the maiden.

As she grew older, she began to spend more time with girls of her own age. Of course I missed her company as I went about my work, but I would never have told her so. I kept myself busy with my own affairs. It was right and natural that she wanted to be with friends, explore the wider world. A mother must let go as her children grow: it would be wrong to try to keep her always by my side. I taught her everything I could and hoped that she would remember half of it. Each generation must make its own mistakes, but surely she had sense enough to keep herself safe.

So when she did not return one afternoon, I was not worried. She had gone with her friends to the meadow where they often went. I could picture them there, laughing as they gathered flowers, talking more quietly as they sat weaving them into garlands. Afterwards they might hitch up their dresses and paddle barefoot at the edge of the river. The sun would loiter to watch them until suddenly it was eventime. Then the shadows would creep out to catch their ankles, and the girls would shriek and giggle as they scampered home. As night fell I placed a candle in the window to guide her through the thickening dusk.

But time passed and still she did not come. At last I went out into the night and traced the way she should have walked. I called her name but there was no answering cry. I passed through the fields and woods, but there was no sign of my daughter. My mind was clogged with fears I dared not unleash. I came to the foot of Mount Etna and kindled a torch from the fires that burn there. I cried until my throat was too hoarse to make a sound. I walked until my steps left smears of blood upon the ground. For nine days and nights I searched, never resting nor eating, but calling for my daughter all the while. Unceasing, refusing to despair, I carried on my search.

Some traces of my beloved daughter I did find. Her girdle lay on the banks of the river, flung there carelessly as if it were no longer needed. The grass in the meadow was flattened, as though a chariot had passed through. An old woman said that she had heard a girl cry out – either in surprise or fear – but she did not know from what direction the cry had come. But there was no other evidence that she had passed that way, or indeed that she had ever existed at all. I wandered from house to house, begging for news of my girl, but the faces at the doors held out no hope. As the days passed I could see that they did not believe my story. There was no evidence of a struggle; only her belt lying discarded in the grass. I had no proof that she had not gone willingly. All that the world could give me now was pity for my loss. My life was shorn of purpose or direction. There is no meaning in the word mother without a child.

At last I returned home, my heart closed tight as a nut. No longer did I wander through the woods and meadows; no longer did the crops and creatures answer to my touch. The weeds grew wild in the gardens, smothering the harvest fruits. The sun beat down hotly on the fields, drying the earth until it cracked. The animals mewled with fear and hunger, desecrating their own beds and fighting amongst each other. I did not care. My daughter was gone and I would not tend the world for any other.

I sat by the well in the centre of Eleusis, bathing my blistered feet. My clothes were stiff with road-dirt; my eyes were red from tiredness. The daughters of Celeus found me there and took pity on me. They led me to their house and showed me their baby brother. His mother was sick and could not nurse him. I held the little boy to my breast and he clung to me. I sang to him in a low voice, as I once sang to my own child. I knew then that my life was not over. My daughter might be gone, but others needed me. I could care for this infant and teach him. I told Celeus that I would nurse the child until his own mother recovered. I would search no more for my missing daughter. There was nothing more to be done or said. I could only wait and hope that one day she would come home.

In the end it was her father who found her. He had his own ways of knowing where to look. Some of his contacts were somewhat shady. He liked to boast of his brother in the under-world. He saw nothing wrong in what had taken place. His own life was always salacious, his relationships vaguely unsavoury. My daughter had been abducted, taken by force. By turning a blind eye, he had implicitly given his permission. To him, it was simply a case of an over-enthusiastic suitor. Arranged marriages can turn out better than love matches, he said; take us as a case in point. I stared at him and looked away. I said nothing.

But maybe I do Zeus an injustice. Did she partly conspire in what took place? Perhaps she confided some private dream to him before she left? Why would a girl want to keep a secret from her mother? Perhaps she thinks that I was never young. Her face when she returned was almost smug. She had tasted forbidden fruit and she had liked it. She told me that she would be returning to her husband soon. She was a grown woman now and had a household of her own. But she would come and visit me again. She smiled at me complicitly and I embraced her.

Life goes on, as they say. I keep myself busy with my work in the fields and meadows. My daughter is a married woman now. She prefers to be known by her given name: Persephone. She seems to be fulfilled in her new life. But I cannot be sure, for I have no part in her realm. But every year, as promised, she comes to visit me. For weeks beforehand, I make ready for her arrival. I clean the world and fill it with spring flowers. We wander across sun-swept slopes and down green valleys. The warm wind stoops to kiss her silken cheeks. Her golden hair swirls lightly round her waist. My daughter smiles at me and takes my hand, and I can dance once more.

******

Think about...

How do you feel when you hear Demeter's story? Is her despair justifiable or is she over-reacting? What experiences have you had which might help you to understand Demeter's position?

What do you think actually happened to Persephone? In what measure was her behaviour appropriate to her age? Was her attitude when she returned reasonable or callous?

Think about your own experience of being mothered. How would you describe your relationship with your mother? What was her relationship with her own mother?

Is there anyone else whom you view as a mother-figure? In what ways have they earned this role?

Think about your own experience of mothering. Do you find responsibility a source of pleasure or frustration? How ready are you to let go when the time for mentoring is done?

Which character do you most identify with, and why?

Task

Think about someone with whom you have a parenting relationship. This could be any child or dependent person in your life. In what ways are you a good parent to them? In what ways could your relationship be improved? Is it enough to be nurturing and supportive? Does a parent need to provide boundaries and enforce these with discipline? Should parents be allowed – or even expected – to have fun too? Does a parent need to be perfect to maintain respect, or could superiority just alienate their charge?

Make a date with this child or dependant. If you don't have one, ask a lonely neighbour round: no-one is ever too old to need a little nurturing. Plan some time together in which you will concentrate on being a 'good-enough' parent to them.

Afterwards think about how your day went. Did you enjoy the experience or find it difficult? What were you pleased about, and what would you do differently next time? Note down your thoughts and reflect on how you could put them into practice.

4. The Wild Woman

Wild women want to have fun. We have one life, and we might as well make the most of it. Wild women run with the wolves. They laugh, love and live life to the full. They are creative, impulsive and innerly beautiful. They are more than a match for the bad boys who sometimes catch their eye. Some people call them selfish, but wild women pay no attention to what others might think. The wild woman neglects her nurturing and procreational functions in favour of more immediate gratification. The good mother may be a pillar of the community, but being a wild woman is much more interesting.

One of the most emotive incarnations of the wild woman is the 'bad mother'. Her figure evokes powerful feelings of frustration or despair. Relationships with our mothers are complex and sometimes painful. We want to love them, but they are not always a benevolent presence in our lives. From earliest infancy their attitude towards us can seem ambiguous. As children we want our mother's affection but fear her anger. We resent correction, even if we deserve to be disciplined. When we are punished we may protect our self-image by deciding that our mother is at fault. The bad mother incarnates our deepest childhood fears of abandonment. Although we reproach her for rejecting us, we fear that she only does so because we are really unworthy of love.[1]

The bad mother is an easy target for our venom. Her selfishness is a clear perversion of natural instinct. The woman who dares to retain her sexual identity after becoming a mother is bitterly criticized: the tabloid press brands her a superficial slut. When Hamlet's mother Gertrude remarries, it precipitates her son's breakdown. Memoirs such as *Mommy Dearest* or *Chinese Cinderella* berate women for their inability to mother properly. What Glenn Close does to the bunny in *Fatal Attraction* is bad mothering. However, the mother's offence can be far less extreme. Spending time or money on yourself is an obvious dereliction of maternal duty. Imelda Marcos squandered her country's resources on hundreds of shoes. It might seem irresponsible, but wild women know they're worth it.

The good mother and the wild woman are of course inversions of the same figure. The Goddess has many incarnations across time and space. Sometimes she appears as protective and nurturing; at others, she is angry or destructive. All her faces are simply aspects of a single underlying reality. Whether we categorize women as either good or bad, we are denying a fundamental part of their feminine identity. The goddess in her darker aspect is revered in her own right in many traditions. When we celebrate this side of life, we acknowledge the interdependence of positive and negative forces. The Great Mother creates life, but she also has the power to take it away. Humans must eat plants or animals in order to live; older generations must die to make way for younger ones. Mother Earth is the source of our sustenance and also our final resting place. Demolition is part of the cycle of creation: pruning is a precursor to fresh growth.[2]

The Great Mother can be kind and nurturing, but at times her face has a darker aspect. The goddess may appear in fearsome form for her own reasons. She may not be angry; she may simply be distracted by other things. No-one warns the young girl what will happen during 'happily ever after'. The interests and activities of her youth are suddenly precluded by more serious responsibilities. Cinderella finds to her horror that after she is married, her ball-gown turns into a straightjacket. The role of wife and mother can become a cage that she feels desperate to escape. Trapped in an archetypal role, she is weighed down by the burden of expectation. The bad mother is defined as one who neglects those in her care: her own needs are not considered in the equation. It seems incredible to us, but she could just want a little time for herself. Mother might turn out to be a woman in her own right after all.

Wild women want to enjoy life, but they may also be searching for deeper personal fulfilment. When apparent success fails to make us happy, we feel guilty and confused. It is difficult to admit that the dream job is not right for us; harder still to let down those whom we love. Marriage or motherhood do not erase the wild woman within us, they just temporarily sublimate it. When we feel frustrated, we blame ourselves for being unrealistic and try to deny the feelings of discontent. Dealing with unacknowledged emotion is like wrestling with a water-bed: the more we push down in one place, the more it swells up elsewhere. It is better to recognize that at times this questioning introspection is normal and natural. The dark goddess is an intrinsic aspect of our femininity. We must each become acquainted with our darker side, if only so that it does not unexpectedly overwhelm us. In spiritual terms, we must all face and integrate our own shadows.

The story of Inanna's descent to the Underworld was found inscribed on clay tablets from Ancient Sumeria. It was a sacred story which would have been declaimed aloud at formal religious ceremonies. Inanna is the Goddess of Love and so she is responsible for fertility on earth. In many ways her story parallels the later Greek myth of Demeter and Persephone, although Inanna combines aspects of both characters. The journey which Inanna undertakes is a more personal one. She is a mature woman who sets off on her travels voluntarily. In terms of personal development, Inanna's dark sister represents her alter ego or other half. In this sense, her journey can be seen as a descent into the psyche in order to integrate the powers of the unconscious mind. Inanna relies initially on the strength of her social self or public persona. She assumes that she can control her instinctive impulses, and this pride is almost her downfall. Ea, to whom her servant Ninshubur appeals for help, is the Lord of Wisdom. Only when his deeper understanding is invoked can the powers of the psyche be fully assimilated.

Inanna's Descent

(A Sumerian Story)

Inanna, the Goddess of Love, left her home in the world above. She went to visit her sister in the dark underworld. Inanna abandoned heaven, abandoned earth, abandoned ladyship. The woman deserted her hearth and her household. She left behind those whom she should have cared for. She set her mind away from the concerns of this world towards the great below. Voluntarily she departed to descend to the lower world.

Inanna set out to visit her sister Ereshkigal, the Queen of the Underworld. She dressed herself carefully for the voyage. She anointed her eyes with dark kohl. She clothed herself in her royal robe, the garment of ladyship and the sign of her status. Over her hair she set a fine cloth, her travelling turban. Around her neck she tied a string of lapis beads. Upon her breast she pinned two shining oval stones. About her waist she fastened a girdle. Around her wrists she placed gold rings. In her hand she took a measuring rod made of lapis lazuli. Thus arrayed in her finery, she set out upon her journey.

The faithful servant Ninshubur accompanied her lady. When they reached the entrance to the Underworld, Inanna bade her stay and wait for her return.

Inanna came to the outer gate and beat upon it.

She called aloud in the voice of command: "Open the gates, for I would enter here."

Neti, the gatekeeper of the nether world, replied: "Who are you, who though still living demands entrance to the land of no return?"

Inanna answered: "I am Inanna. I come to visit my sister, the Queen of the Underworld. Her husband has died and she is all alone."

Neti the gatekeeper sent word to Ereshkigal of her visitor. The dark queen bit her lip; it turned the colour of tamarind. She frowned and gave her stern reply:

"Let her enter naked and bowed low, as do all who enter here. If she would enter, she must obey the laws of the Underworld. She will be subject to my decrees."

Neti returned to his place and drew back the bolts. The gates of the Underworld swung open. Inanna placed her foot upon the path which each must travel alone.

When she passed through the first gate, Inanna's headdress was taken from her. Her hair was exposed and she was unprotected.

She asked, "Pray, gatekeeper, what is this?"

Neti replied, "My lady, go on your way. These are the rites decreed by the gods. Do not question the ways of the Underworld."

As she passed through the second gate, the string of lapis beads was removed from her neck. Her beautiful adornment was taken from her.

Inanna asked, "Pray, gatekeeper, what is this?"

Neti answered, "My lady, these are the rules decreed by the gods. Do not question the ways of the Underworld."

At the third gate, the shining oval stones were removed from her breast.

Inanna asked, "Pray, gatekeeper, what is this?"

Neti replied, "These are the laws decreed by the gods. Do not question the ways of the Underworld."

The signs of womanhood were taken from her body. There is no place for such things in the Underworld.

At the fourth gate, the girdle was removed from her waist. She had no place to keep her keys: her responsibilities were taken from her. There is no need for such things in the Underworld.

At the fifth gate, the gold rings were removed from around her wrists. Her finery was taken from her. At the sixth gate, the measuring rod of lapis was seized from her hand. The power of a ruler was taken from her. At the seventh gate, the royal garment was stripped from her body. Her regal status was taken from her.

Naked and unadorned, Inanna came before the Queen of the Underworld.

Ereshkigal was seated in splendour in the great hall. Beside her sat the Annuna, the seven judges of the Underworld. Inanna stood proudly before her sister. She bade her sister rise from her seat: she would have taken took her sister's place upon the throne. The Annuna looked upon Inanna with wrath at her presumption. Their voices proclaimed her guilt. Their judgement was the judgement of death. Ereshkigal would not spare her sister from the laws of that realm. Inanna sickened; she writhed in pain; she died. Her body was hung from a hook upon the wall.

The loyal Ninshubur waited for three days and three nights at the gates of the Underworld. When her lady did not return, Ninshubur went to the gods and begged for help. She filled the heavens with her wailings and her pleas. Her hair was covered with ash. She wore a single garment like a beggar. The world joined in her mourning for the Goddess of Love. On earth no animal lay with its mate; no man met his wife. The sun turned his face from the barren land. Clouds lay over the whole of creation.

The gods heard the commotion and were disturbed, but none would help Inanna in her plight. Ninshubur came at last to Ea the Allfather, the Lord of Wisdom. Ea heard her pleas and he was troubled. He took the dirt from beneath his fingernails and he fashioned two *kurgurra*, sexless creatures who could travel safely in the nether regions. "Go," he told them. "Bring comfort to Ereshkigal."

The *kurgurra* came to where Ereshkigal sat alone in the darkness. Her hair was loose and her breasts were bare: she moaned and writhed upon her throne. The *kurgurra* asked after her welfare and she told them of her pain. In her loneliness she was glad to see them, for they comforted her. She asked what boon they desired and they requested the body hanging from a hook on the wall. The *kurgurra* sprinkled the body with water of life, so Inanna awoke. She rose from the dead and her sister looked kindly upon her.

Inanna had to return to her duties in the world above. She ascended the pathway from the Underworld. As she passed through each gate, her finery was restored to her. By her side walked a crowd of *galla*, demons seeking another to take her place in the lower kingdom. As they came to the world of light, the demons took hold of Ninshubur.

"No," said Inanna. "She has been my faithful messenger. You shall not have her to take my place in the Underworld."

They passed through the upper land and the demons sought another to take Inanna's place. Everywhere the world rejoiced to see the Queen of Heaven return. Inanna would not let the demons take any who had mourned in her absence. At last she came to her home and entered the palace. Dumuzi, the king, lay upon his couch arrayed in fine clothes. Slave-girls played pipes whilst he feasted and drank. Inanna fixed her faithless husband with the eye of death. She spoke coldly to the demons:

"You shall have him to take my place in the Underworld."

The demons seized Dumuzi and dragged him away forthwith. He screamed and begged for mercy, but the demons knew no pity. Dumuzi took Inanna's place with Ereshkigal in the Underworld.

Inanna gazed upon her consort's empty seat and her heart was heavy. The Goddess of Love mourned for her lost companion. She had no spirit for her work in the world. Inanna sat upon her throne and her face was dark. Musicians played a sad tune with a slow refrain. The mourners wept and rent their clothes. In her grief, Dumuzi's sister Geshtinanna came before the queen. She begged permission to take her brother's place for half the year. Inanna lifted Geshtinanna up and accepted her offer. Thus it came to pass that Dumuzi returns to the world each spring. The Queen of Love is reunited with her husband and life continues.

****

Think about...

Why do you think Inanna sets out on this journey? What might she hope to gain from her experience? Is the reward worth the price paid?

What might the articles which Inanna has to surrender symbolize, in terms of her worldly identity? What remains after she has given up these external attributes?

Are Inanna's actions justified, or does she neglect her responsibilities? How does her story resonate with your image of a 'bad mother'? Who has been a 'bad mother' in your experience? How has this affected you?

What things might make you want to leave your current life? What might attract you to a new way of being? What keeps you where you are? Are you content with this state of affairs?

What personal qualities might Inanna's 'dark sister' represent? Are these necessarily bad? What are the characteristics of your 'dark twin'? Who knows this other side of you?

Task

Your life is transient, but you imbue it with meaning through your thought and memories. In order to access the wisdom of the unconscious, Inanna has to surrender her sense of self. What would you have to leave behind, if you made a similar journey?

Collect some objects which represent the things you cherish in life. These things will not necessarily have any financial value, but they should be of emotional significance. They might be things like a silver ring; a smooth beach pebble; a photograph, and so on. Put these objects in a special place where you can see them easily. Meditate upon their significance: are you paying enough attention to the important things in your life?

Make a 'life box' – this could be a carved wooden casket or a decorated shoe box – where you can keep your objects safely. You may wish to include a note or poem reminding you of what each item represents. Make a note in your diary to look inside your life box on your birthday and add any new objects you want to.

5. The Grandmother

We often meet grandmothers in myths and fairy tales. Usually they appear near the beginning of the adventure; typically they offer the hero or heroine good advice. We instinctively feel that we can trust this guidance. Grandmother is generally portrayed as a wise old woman. Gentle and kindly, she may take the place of an absent mother. She is a constant source of sympathy and support. Her experience of life means that her opinion, especially of human nature, is well-founded. In addition she often holds a vast repository of woman's knowledge: she is a herbalist, a healer and a storyteller.[1]

There are very few stories in which Grandmother is the central character. The wise storyteller knows her audience: what the youngsters want are figures with whom they can identify. Those that do feature her tend to be tangential or anecdotal. Red Riding Hood is on the way to visit her grandmother's house in the woods: the old woman represents, among other things, her own future self. Widow Betsy Ross is credited with having sewn the first American flag. The 'Stars and Stripes' was probably designed by someone else, but popular imagination requires a venerable mother to stand beside the founding fathers.

There is another reason why we have so few stories about kind elderly women. Grandmother is not as old as she seems. The years have gone so fast, she can hardly credit it. Inside, she sometimes feels scarcely older than her granddaughter. If a wolf knocked at her door, she would get him to take her out for dinner. The mirror confirms that in a good light she can still look beautiful. She stands, stately and serene, feeling the riches of wisdom within her. Surely the image with whom she should identify is not the crone, but the queen.

However, the queen in post-matriarchal society finds herself in difficult circumstances. Kings of any age are viewed as virile figures, for they embody the fertility of the land. If their consort dies they are expected to take a new wife. Men are encouraged to remain sexually active, for they can father a child at any age. By contrast, older women are viewed with some ambivalence. They are no longer assessed in terms of their ability to attract a mate. They have passed the age of childbearing, and their physical strength is starting to decline. Whilst they are usually treated with respect, their opinions may be seen as out-of-date and consequently redundant. If they are outspoken they may be perceived as strident and domineering. The grandmother in modern society is often an anomalous figure. Long-distance phone calls assure her of affection, but she is effectively excluded from the important matters of life.[2]

Some cultures accord more respect to the wisdom of experience. Women can live long after their productive and reproductive functions are complete. During this extended period of life they become primarily a source of knowledge for the community. Through their stories, the elderly are venerated for their contribution to the tribe. These are typically pre-technical societies in which the complementary contributions of male and female, youth and age are honoured and celebrated. This attitude of appreciation is typical of the aboriginal people of Australia and the indigenous inhabitants of North America. The following story is based on a legend of the Brule Sioux, a Plains Indian people, but the events take place far to the south in the desert lands of New Mexico. The medicine plant in the story is peyote, which is credited with both physical healing and spiritual insights. It plays an important part in vision quests including the sweat lodge ritual.

Grandmother and the Medicine Plant

(A Native American Legend)

Long ago, there lived a people who made their home on the edge of the desert. It was a hard life, since by day the sun beat down upon them and there was little food to find. But the land was beautiful and there were few wild beasts apart from the coyote who howled in the desert at night. The people knew the secret of cultivating maize, the speckled corn which the gods had given them, and they rarely suffered from hunger.

One day a sickness came to the people. Their skins became covered in sweat, their eyes rolled up in their heads and their tongues thickened so that they were unable to speak. The people had never known such an affliction before, and many died from it. Now, there lived amongst the people an old woman who was wise in the ways of healing. She had not seen an illness like this, and she knew that her medicines were of no use against it. On the fourth day of the sickness, she took her granddaughter and fled away into the desert.

They walked all morning, and the vegetation grew thinner as the sands grew wider. Their shadows grew shorter and came to play around their ankles. There was no place to hide from the hot rays of the midday sun. At last they stopped to rest beside a pile of rocks. Grandmother took out her water-skin and some corn cakes, which she gave to the girl.

"Grandmother, are you not hungry?"

"I am old, my child. I do not need as much food as you."

In the afternoon a great bird came and circled high above them. It was an eagle, lord of the skies, and its coming was a good omen. Grandmother raised her arms to the bird and prayed that they might find knowledge to save themselves and their people. The bird flew off towards the west, where the sun hastened down to the horizon. Grandmother and the girl struggled after it until their moccasins were worn. They stopped at last beside a large cactus. It was a great green globe with sixteen segments, covered in tufts of thorns. By this time it was nearly nightfall, and darkness drew across the sky like a blanket. The spiny plant did not provide much shelter, but the old woman dug a hollow in the sand. She collected dry saguara ribs and built a small fire, sheltered from the wind. The girl lay down but Grandmother wrapped herself in her blanket and sat erect, gazing out into the night.

"Grandmother, are you not tired?"

"I am old, my child. I do not need as much sleep as you."

The air grew chill and somewhere in the desert, Coyote howled to the moon. Grandmother sat with her eyes wide, staring out into the night. Her mind grew blank and she began to dream. In her vision she heard a voice speaking to her.

"I have medicine which can help you."

Grandmother jerked upright. She had heard the words clearly, but no-one was there. Perhaps it was the spirits of the desert who had spoken to her. She pulled the blanket tightly around her and straightened her back. She sat with her eyes wide, staring out across the sands.

"I have medicine which can help you."

Grandmother shook her head crossly. Again she had heard the words, and again no-one was to be seen. The moon-shadows had swung round across the sand. She must have been sleeping after all. Grandmother poked the embers of the fire. She hunched her old bones close to catch the faint warmth. She swayed backwards and forwards, trying to catch the meaning of the dream.

"I have medicine which can help you."

Grandmother raised her head and saw first light in the sky. Her granddaughter opened her eyes and looked at the great cactus. Grandmother saw a small cactus reflected in the girl's eyes. Finally she understood who had been talking to her in the night.

She knew what to do, but still she was careful. Taking her bone knife, she cut off one of the green segments. She squeezed a drop of the juice onto her tongue. It tasted good; it did not sting or burn her mouth. She cut a small strip of flesh and placed it in her mouth. Carefully she chewed it four times, then spat it out. She felt refreshed and invigorated, but still she waited to be sure. Finally she took a piece of the plant and swallowed it. The feelings of wellbeing increased and she knew that this was the medicine she sought. She experienced knowledge and under-standing and inner vision. Ceremonially she cut small green buttons off the sacred plant. She spoke to her granddaughter:

"Taste this new herb and pray with me. It has no mouth, but it is telling me many things."

At first Grandmother was worried that there would not be enough of this new medicine for her people. Then she heard many small voices calling to her. They were medicine plants calling to her from their hiding places amongst the chaparral and thorn bushes. The old woman and the girl picked the sacred buttons and filled the hide bag with them.

Grandmother and granddaughter set off towards their home. Although they had no more food or water, the medicine kept them strong-hearted and strong-minded. When they came amongst their tribe, people were happy to see them but many were still sick. Grandmother told the people:

"I have a new medicine which will make you well."

Guided by the spirits, she taught them how to use the holy herb. Under her instruction the men built a round house of willow sticks covered with animal skins. In the centre of the floor they lit a fire set around with stones. Everybody ate four buttons of the sacred plant. The people themselves became inspired by the new medicine. One man took a gourd rattle and started to shake it. Another seized a drum and began to beat in time with the song. The old woman brought cool fresh water in a skin bag and everyone drank; she sprinkled some on the hot stones and the tipi filled with steam. Inspired by the spirits, someone shaped the embers of the fire into the shape of a water bird. The people prayed to the four cardinal directions of the land, giving thanks to the Great Spirit who had spoken through the medicine plant. A man threw green cedar on the fire and its fragrant smoke was the breath of all growing things. In this way the first medicine ceremony was devised. The people were nourished in body and spirit, and the sick amongst them were cured. From them the worship of the sacred plant spread to all the tribes of the land. Thus did Grandfather Peyote make himself known and come to the hearts of the people.

****

Think about...

Why do you think this story was originally told? What does the story explain? What instructions does it give? What other things can we learn from the story?

How does Grandmother behave, and why? What benefits does this bring – to herself? To her immediate family? To the wider community? What message does this give to us, the audience?

What relationships does this story examine? Which archetypal figures appear in the story? Which character do you most identify with, and why? If this is your role, which people in your life play complementary parts? How do you feel about these relationships?

Task

Life is a tapestry woven of many different coloured threads. It is only when you look back that you can see patterns in our lives. Often the true significance of an event only becomes apparent afterwards. Your experiences so far have made you the person you are today. The wise old woman can pass on this legacy of life lessons.

What have you inherited from your grandmother? Do you look like her, or have similar interests? Did she leave you anything of value?

Find something that reminds you of your grandmother. This could be a picture or an object which symbolizes her legacy to you. Place this in front of you as you do the following meditation.

Imagine that you are eighty years old. As this older self, think back over your life. How have things turned out? What did you achieve between your actual age and now? What interests did you follow and what dreams did you pursue? What practical steps did you take to make things happen? What are you proudest of, and what dangers did you avoid? What is important to you at this stage of your life? What advice would you like to give your younger self?

You can draw on the wisdom of the grandmother. Think of a problem which you are currently facing. Write a letter to your older self, briefly stating the issue and asking for help. Put down the pen and close your eyes briefly. Then write back to your self, giving advice and encouragement. You may be surprised at what you discover. Keep this letter somewhere safe and re-read it in a few days. Honour the wisdom of your older self by expressing thanks and appreciation.

6. The Wicked Witch

The witch is a familiar figure from children's fairy tales. Despite her wickedness we know her well and she is reassuringly easy to recognize. Hunch-backed and hooked-nosed, she wears a black cape and tall black hat. She rides through the skies on her broomstick accompanied by her familiar, usually a black cat. Living alone in her cottage in the dark woods, she concocts evil brews in her cauldron. Sometimes she convenes with other witches in covens of thirteen to dance by the light of the moon. There are rumours that she eats small children: certainly she destroys footballs landing in her garden. Our mothers have warned us about her and we stay well away... until one day we find ourselves accidentally at her door.

On closer acquaintance, however, we will find that the witch is not so alarming after all. Her features are just those of an elderly woman; her attributes reflect the ancient worship of the great goddess. The negative connotations of these characteristics reflect the way in which we are afraid of things which we do not understand. The witch's bent back and prominent nose are natural products of the ageing process. Having outlived most of her contemporaries, the crone befriends a creature normally associated with farmyard duties. Living alone with few possessions, she has to work to support herself. Fortunately she has acquired a little life experience along the way: her knowledge of herbs makes her invaluable as a village healer and midwife. Her cauldron recalls the Celtic 'Cauldron of Life', providing endless nourishment and capable of regenerating those who fall into it. Her broomstick is an ancient fertility symbol, combining a phallic stick with a female brush. Black is the colour of the night: it is associated with concealment, but also with the moon and feminine mysteries. The coven of thirteen reflects a sisterhood of priestesses, their number determined by the tally of lunar months in a year.[1]

The witch is usually portrayed as wicked, because those who fear her power cannot imagine that she might use it for unselfish ends. Her ugliness is perceived as a physical embodiment of her inner malignancy. However, we can choose to see the witch from a different perspective. The witch is the counterpart of the grand-mother: she is her dark sister, and as such may be seen as another aspect of the self. The character of the crone rightly includes both figures, in the same way that the great goddess encompasses both creation and destruction. Darkness is simply the inverse to light: both aspects are potentially present in each of us. In *The Wizard of Oz* there are both good and bad witches; the musical *Wicked* explores the factors which made childhood friends adopt these opposing roles. When we first encounter the old woman she is a neutral figure, with no reason for either evil or kind intent. As Shakespeare said, there is nothing either good or bad, but thinking makes it so. By projecting malign motives onto the 'wicked' witch we force her to act in a way that confirms our hypothesis. Conversely, we may ascribe good intentions to the sorceress by calling her a 'white' witch. When we understand the archetypes properly, we can see that neither ameliorating adjective is necessary.

Sometimes the ugliness of the crone is simply a ploy to test those she encounters before she reveals her inner worth. In the Celtic tale of Niall Noighiallach, the four older brothers refuse to give the hideous hag at the well a kiss in exchange for a draught of water. Good-natured young Niall does so willingly and when he opens his eyes is rewarded by the sight of a beautiful woman. She represents the spirit of the land: through union with her, Niall and his descendants ultimately obtain the kingship of Ireland. This theme is reversed in the story of Shrek, whose princess turns out to look reassuringly like himself.

In Russian folklore the crone is often named as Baba Yaga. Usually portrayed as a witch, she can be benevolent if so disposed. She lives alone deep in the forest and the bones of her victims form the fence that surrounds her house. This place marks the boundary between the worlds of the living and the dead. She is said to have control over the Sun and his children, Day and Night. The dead should always be buried just before sunset, so that the Sun can carry away the departing soul on his downward journey. In another aspect, she is guardian of the fountain which supplies the Water of Life. It is apparent from these surviving details that Baba Yaga was originally a powerful fertility goddess with control over life and death. Although demoted by Christianity in favour of Mary, who in turn was ousted by the atheism of the Communist regime, vestiges of her authority survive. Figures in Russian folk tales show layers of influence, like *babushka* dolls: Christian, pagan, shamanistic and psychological perspectives all contribute to the potency of the narrative.[2]

In the following story, the young girl is naturally afraid of the old woman who lives in the woods. She has heard tales which render the witch a figure to be feared. In addition, her personal experiences of strange women indicate that they are often motivated by malice. Nonetheless, by listening to her doll she is able to access deeper knowledge. In order to grow up Vasilisa must learn to look beyond surface appearances and trust her own inner judgement. She ventures into the unknown but what she finds there is empowering because it develops her own innate potential. Once she has learned to believe in herself, she is able to take control of her own life.

Baba Yaga
Or, The Witch in the Woods

(A Russian Folktale)

Once there lived a girl called Vasilisa. It is a common name, but this girl was uncommon on account of her exceptional beauty. For this reason she was known as Vasilisa the Beautiful. Vasilisa was the daughter of a wealthy merchant, and when she was young her life was free of any troubles. However, when she was just eight years old her mother became seriously ill. The woman knew from her experience that she did not have long to live. She called Vasilisa to her bedside and gave her a wonderful doll, so carefully carved and finely clothed that it seemed almost alive.

"Take this doll and feed it like a child," she told her daughter. "It will help you whenever you are in need."

A few days later the mother died and shortly afterwards the merchant married again. His new wife was a widow with two daughters of her own. Vasilisa was pleased at the prospect of having sisters, but she soon came to regret the change. At first her stepmother seemed kind, but as Vasilisa grew she became jealous of the girl's beauty. Since the merchant was often away on business he did not realize what was happening in his house. The stepmother gave Vasilisa the dirtiest and most difficult jobs, but the girl never seemed to suffer from her hard work. This was because the doll did all the work for her, leaving Vasilisa free to wander in the fields around the house. However, sometimes it is better not to have too much time to think; and the girl was often unhappy when she remembered her own dear mother and how kind she had been.

Seven years passed and Vasilisa grew into a fair young woman. Since she was always dressed in rags and had no mirror, she had no idea of her beauty. She wandered in the meadows each day whilst the doll performed her chores; but she was careful never to enter the thick forest which stood behind the house, for it was said to be inhabited by a witch. This woman, Baba Yaga, was wise in the ways of plants and animals. She could weave a spell to make your crops flourish, or conjure a curse to curdle the blood in your veins. She could concoct a love philtre to make your dreams come true, or charge you for a charm to offset the effects of her own dubious doings. She made amulets to avert the evil eye and mixed medicines which brought unnatural relief. It was said moreover that she could speak to the spirits, and that day and night were her servants and heeded her command. For this reason the people of those parts left her alone unless they needed her services. None liked the witch and many feared her: for men are often afraid of what they do not understand.

The stepmother and her daughters saw how lovely Vasilisa had become, and they hated her all the more. She never complained to her father of their treatment for fear of making him unhappy. One autumn day the merchant was away and the stepmother resolved to be rid of the girl once and for all. Whilst Vasilisa was walking, she let the fire in the stove go out and made sure that there was no dry tinder in the house. When Vasilisa returned the stepmother shouted at her angrily and told her to go and find a light. Pushing the girl out of the house, she slammed the door behind her. It was growing late and Vasilisa was very frightened. Luckily she had her doll tucked inside her dress. The doll told her to seek help from Baba Yaga, the old woman who lived in the woods behind the house. Knowing that she was safe so long as she had her mother's doll, the poor girl set out towards the dark woods.

Vasilisa walked for hours until it was almost dark. Clutching her doll, she went deeper and deeper into the forest. There were no proper paths, only faint tracks made by wild animals. At last she came to an open space and the sight she saw froze her feet to the ground. In front of her was a fence which gleamed white in the darkness: it was constructed entirely of bones. Atop each fence post was a human skull and the eye sockets glowed so brightly that they lit up the clearing like torches. The gateway was barred by two crossed legs, the bolts of the gate were human hands, and the lock was a mouth full of sharp teeth. In the middle of the clearing was a small wooden hut which turned slowly towards Vasilisa as she looked. To her horror, she saw that it was perched on top of four chicken legs.

Just at that moment there was a terrible commotion and Baba Yaga herself came into view. She was riding in a mortar which she rowed with a pestle, sweeping away all traces of her passage with a wicker broom. The gate swung open when it heard its mistress approaching, but Baba Yaga had seen her visitor and stopped short. Vasilisa would gladly have turned and run, but the doll told her not to be afraid. In any case there was nowhere to hide, so she bravely stood her ground and told the old woman her story.

When Baba Yaga heard her request, she looked calculatingly upon Vasilisa.

"I will gladly help you", she said, "But first you must work for me. I have no-one to care for my house whilst I am out in the woods. Clean and cook for three days, and the fire is yours."

Vasilisa had heard fearsome stories of the witch in the woods and was convinced that she would be eaten at the end of this time. However, the doll advised her to stay and do as she was asked. Each day Baba Yaga went out into the forest to collect tokens for her talismans and herbs for her potions. Whilst she was gone the doll cleaned the house and performed all the tasks which were set for the girl. The only job left for Vasilisa was cooking the supper, which the doll was too small to do because she might fall into the fire. For the first time in her life Vasilisa had to do some work herself, and she found that she actually enjoyed it.

On the third evening Baba Yaga told the girl that she had

worked well and was free to go. Leading Vasilisa to the gate, she took down one of the skulls with glowing eyes and placed it upon a wooden pole. Vasilisa took this fearsome torch and made her way back through the forest. She was surprised to find that the journey did not take very long in this direction. She came to her father's house and knocked on the door. The stepmother came out with her daughters, and when the skull saw them it stared so hard that they were all burned to a cinder. Vasilisa buried the skull carefully in the garden and went into the house.

The next day the merchant sent word for his family to join him in town for a great party to celebrate the czar's son's birthday. Now that her stepmother was gone, Vasilisa had plenty of fine clothes to wear and no-one to make her stay at home. When the prince saw Vasilisa at the festivities he was overcome by her beauty and asked her to be his wife. They married and lived happily together, and when the old czar died the prince inherited his throne. Vasilisa often visited her childhood home and walked in the dark woods which stood behind the house, but she never saw the old woman again.

******

Think about...

When do you think this story was first told? How might it have changed over time? What other stories does it remind you of? What might the story be trying to tell us?

Which other archetypal figures appear in the story? How do they relate to one another?

Whose voice is speaking through the doll? Why do we internalize the opinions of others in this way? In your experience, do these 'voices' help or hinder your judgement?

Where have you met the archetype of the witch in your own life? How did this experience affect you? In retrospect, were you fears justified? How do you feel about this person now?

Can you identify with the figure of the witch? In what ways and circumstances might this help you? How could you draw on the power of the witch to achieve positive ends?

Task

You can draw on the wisdom of the witch to empower your own life. In this task you will create a charm which has nothing supernatural about it. By affirming what is good in your life, you simply give yourself the confidence to operate effectively in the world. Using the law of attraction through possession of similar properties is known as 'sympathetic magic'.

Certain things are traditionally seen as lucky. Crossing your fingers brings good fortune, as does touching wood or seeing a black cat walk across your path; breaking a mirror means seven years' bad luck... unless you quickly avert it by throwing salt over your shoulder. Whether you believe in it or not, you have probably done something similarly superstitious at some point in your life.

Collect some 'lucky' talismans. Depending on your personal beliefs, these might include a four-leaved clover; a sprig of white heather; a wishbone; a quartz crystal; a tiny model of a cat; a silver pendant and so on. You will also need a very small cloth bag on a long drawstring. You may want to make this yourself: choose the finest fabric that you can find, such as a fragment of embroidered silk on a fine cord. Select some of your talismans to make your charm. The objects chosen should be combined in a way that has meaning for you. Put these talismans into your bag and tie it shut. Wear your charm around your neck, preferably concealed inside your clothing to retain all its power. If you are feeling especially generous (or slightly cynical) make your charm for a friend. The power of gift will render it effective even if neither of you believes in magic!

You might also like at this point to explore the exercise for the last archetypal figure, the Ogre, who is the counterpart of the Wicked Witch.

Male Archetypes: The Great Journey

Boys will be boys. Much to the consternation of their mothers, no amount of gender-neutral activity can divert them from male concerns. These may include shooting (any stick can be a gun); football (the kicked object need not be round); and wrestling (no equipment needed at all). Girls exit the school playground in chattering pairs; small boys are attached to any passing ball by invisible pieces of elastic. Whilst this observation is a generalization, the same tendencies persist into later life. Whether because of nature or nurture, men are expected to cope with confrontation in the workplace and on the sports field; women are thought to be somehow better at nurturing, and are often responsible for running the household even if they also hold down a full-time job.[1]

Modern men find themselves in a difficult position. They are genetically programmed to take risks and behave competitively, but they will be penalized if they exhibit disruptive behaviour. Boys must learn how to balance these conflicting demands and behave in a socially acceptable manner. The most reliable way of developing appropriate behaviour patterns is by imitating successful adults. As children, the first example we get is from parents or parental figures who provide an image of correct conduct. As we grow older, stories supply a supplementary or alternative source of role models. We may encounter these stories through books, films or plays but the tales they tell are based on older patterns.

The most widespread source of male role-model is the hero-myth. Many boys experience a vague sense of questing impulse, or life purpose. For some, this will develop into a vocation such as medicine or priesthood. For others it will transform into a spirit of enquiry, whether working in the sciences or prospecting an oil field. The popularity of survival adventure programmes on television testifies to the universality of this impulse. The hero is often identified with the sun, whose trajectory represents a voyage of discovery or exploration. At the end of his mission, the hero is irrevocably transformed. Each quest the hero undertakes therefore constitutes a rite of passage. Despite his prominence, the hero is nonetheless only one of the male archetypes. Other manifestations – the young boy, the old man – are equally important components of the masculine psyche.

Male archetypes are linked by the concept of a heroic quest. The different episodes of the hero's adventure reflect sequential stages of his life. The small boy has to rely upon his wits and good fortune; the young man depends on physical prowess; and the old man calls upon his experience and cunning. Within this triumvirate, the most influential figure is the hero, for the stage of adulthood occupies most of a man's life. The wise old man or sage plays a supporting role in the hero's story, proffering good advice as he sets off on his journey. Although not often biologically related, he is a father figure and so represents another aspect of the impetuous hero himself.

At each life stage the male archetypal figure has a clear counterpart, or alter ego. Whereas the female characters shift and mingle, the male is traditionally defined as either hero or villain. In this world-view it is always either dark or light: there is no recognition that day must cede to night, and will in turn prevail. We must recognize that one archetype is simply the reverse side of the other: they are both eternally present and intrinsically interchangeable. Some people fear that they will be overwhelmed by the negative side of their personality, like Dr Jekyll with Mr Hyde. In truth, the dark face is nothing but the light face in relief: by recognizing and honouring it, we reclaim the balance of powers that is our birthright.

7. The Infant Prince

As infants we arrive in the world full of hope. We open our eyes and squint at the brightness of the light. We cry out and our mother responds to our needs even before we have analyzed the source of discomfort. We seek succour, and it is provided. We defecate, and we are cleansed. We sleep, and nothing disturbs us until we wake refreshed. No wonder that this state of affairs is often depicted as Paradise, the original condition of mankind. Whether or not it reflects individual experience, this is the primal peace from which any later deviation is by definition a fall.

In every culture the child is a symbol of innocence. His fresh face represents natural simplicity and spontaneity. Our hopes for him are partly vicarious: potentially he can fulfil all our disappointed dreams. The child lives in the present, without worries or regrets. The Taoists view this state as one of the most desirable of human characteristics, perfectly complementing the wisdom of age. Hindu tradition terms childhood *balya*, a state of mind analogous to life in Paradise before mankind acquired knowledge of good and evil. The image of the child often marks the conquest of some inner anxiety and the subsequent attainment of inner peace.

Every child is unique. Most of us were lucky enough to be loved and cherished as children. In a very deep sense this makes us each feel somehow special. The sense of being exceptional is one of the most important gifts which our parents can give us. It is directly related to our psychological health and sense of security in later life. This feeling of stability does not preclude experimenting with different roles and experiences. One of the ways in which we can do this safely is through stories. When we hear a story, we usually identify with the main character. When the hero turns out to be of royal blood, our sense of being special is confirmed by this discovery.

The foundling is a unique category of child. Arriving without family ties, he is not burdened by precedents and preconceptions. Most children receive positive support from their fathers and mothers, but it is hard not to be affected by parental expectations. Even when our parents' hopes are in line with our own wishes they can seem oppressive, especially during adolescence. The foundling has no expectations to confirm or confound: he is free to make his own choices. Without the weight of vicarious dreams, he can do whatever he wants with his life. He may not inherit a fortune but the world will provide him with what he needs. His legacy is a clean start, untainted by the sins of his fathers. In a patriarchal society where blood feuds are inherited, this is an especially fortunate state of affairs.

When the foundling arrives there is no clue to his identity but his behaviour shows him to be of noble blood. As events reveal his true heritage, his claim to the crown is vindicated by both deportment and descent. His ascent to the throne depicts the rightful marriage of nature and nurture, the outcome of fate and circumstance. The aura of exaltation can be invoked by outsiders in wider circumstances too. A royal legacy was often claimed by an upstart king to validate his sovereignty. The long-lost regent grandfather may have been a spiritual, rather than a sanguinal, ancestor but the royal right of succession ensured that the new incumbent was officially acceptable to his priests and people.

There are many stories of foundlings who turn out to be of noble descent. Little Fauntleroy and Tarzan both find that they come from aristocratic English families. In these stories character always triumphs over condition: the innate conduct of the child proves their true worth. Young Washington cannot tell a lie. Oliver Twist's ineptness as a thief leads to his reunion with his grandfather. Sometimes the child's special status is known, but only to those responsible for his welfare: Jesus Christ and Krishna were both born into lowly circumstances. In other cases it is their conduct as young men which leads to their eventual recognition. Paris was raised by a shepherd as his son: he returned to Troy for a sporting competition and won every event. Romulus and Remus were suckled by a she-wolf: when brought before the king they were recognized as his heirs. Moses was found in a basket of bullrushes and brought up in Pharoah's house: he proceeded to lead his people out of slavery.[1]

The story of Sargon is older, but has a comparable theme. Sargon of Akkad, who ruled from c.2335-2279BC, was born of obscure parentage but rose to found the first empire the world had ever seen. He came to power in Mesopotamia, in the land that is now called Iraq. The region between the Tigris and Euphrates rivers was the cradle of Western civilization. Sumer, to the south, was a wide fertile plain with few trees. Here people learned to grow food crops and built permanent settlements. These grew into walled cities with a temple at the centre, surrounded by farmland. Each city-state was governed by an independent king who administered his estate on behalf of the gods. To the north was the land of Akkad, named after the language of its inhabitants. Here Sargon founded his new capital city of Agade (Arcadia). The story of Sargon's birth and childhood is given in a Sumerian text purporting to be his biography; his rule is confirmed in the Sumerian king lists. Later incidents are detailed in other Sumerian sources including the Chronicle of Early Kings. Sargon is claimed by some scholars to be the source for the Biblical figure of Nimrod.

Sargon the Great

(An Akkadian Story)

They say that my father was a gardener. It is an apt analogy, for I have indeed tended this land well. But I contend that my real father La'ibum was of royal blood and I can therefore rightly be called Sargon, the true king.

My mother was a high priestess of Azipiranu. She conceived me in secret and bore me in silence. She set me in a basket of rushes, softly lined with finest linen. She sealed the lid with bitumen and cast it into the river Euphrates. The waters of the river bore me up and carried me to safety. The basket came to the edge of the river at Kish and was cast up on the shore. There I was found at daybreak by Akki, who had come to the river to draw water. He took me to his house and raised me as his own son. There I grew and flourished, and when the time came he trained me to be a gardener.

I worked in the temple gardens and I learned my craft well. Labouring each day under the caresses of Shamash the sun, I grew strong and skilful. There Inanna spied me as I grew to manhood. The goddess of love came to me one day and demanded that I grant her my favour. Who was I to reject her advances? I gave Inanna what she desired, and for four years I was a lord in her embrace.

The gods sent a vision to Ur-Zababa, the king of Kish. Ur-Zababa dreamt of me before we met. He saw me as I worked in the temple gardens and he knew me from his dream. He desired to talk with me and he sent for me to come to his chambers. I understood his dream and explained its meaning to him. Ur-Zababa was pleased and looked kindly on me. He appointed me to be his cup-bearer. Now I no longer laboured in the gardens: I attended the king and became his right-hand man.

One night Inanna sent a vision to me. In my dream she sent

the king into the waters of the river and he did not come out. I told the king about my dream and he was afraid. He sent for the chief smith to have me killed, but Inanna forbade it. The king became even more frightened. He sent me to Uruk carrying a clay tablet for his brother-king Lugal-Zage-Si. The tablet bore a message asking Lugal to dispose of me. Lugal set me many challenges, hoping that I would die, but I accomplished all of them. In fury I returned to Kish, to the king who had been a father to me. I did not raise my hand against Ur-Zababa. I did not spill one drop of royal blood. The vision sent by Inanna came to pass. He entered the waters and he did not come out. The people of Kish knew me and hailed me as their king.

I took revenge on those who had thought to work against me. I captured Uruk and razed its great walls to the ground. I brought Lugal in a dog-collar to the gates of the city. I marched on Kazallu and turned it into a heap of ruins, so that there was not even a perch for a bird to stand on. I conquered all of Sumeria and washed my weapons in the lower sea. I chose governors from amongst my own people to share my table and administer the smaller kingdoms. I founded my new city in the north on the left bank of the Euphrates and named it Agade.

In all Sumeria I had neither rival nor equal: I ruled over the black-headed people. My soldiers were armed with mighty axes of bronze. I ascended the upper mountains; I burst through the lower mountains. I came to Elam in the east. In the eleventh year of my reign I conquered the western land to its farthest point. I secured Amanus, the cedar forest, and Taurus, the silver mountain. I established trade routes so that wood and silver could be floated freely down the river. I brought it all under one authority and ruled it in its entirety. I set up my statues every- where and caused inscriptions to be written on my monuments. Mine was a kingdom of kingdoms and truly I was the first king of kings.

In all my achievements I took care never to forget the gods. I ruled the cities through the favour of their patron deities. Although I destroyed the walls of Uruk, yet I was careful to respect the temples of Anu and his daughter Inanna. Indeed, I was anointed high priest of Anu, sky-father of the gods. My daughter Enheduanna is a priestess of Nanna, the moon-god of Ur. Her great hymn, the Exaltation of Inanna, will forever proclaim the greatness of the goddess of love. I have instructed the scribes to put images from the myths alongside the writing on their clay tablets. In this way, everyone can see the significance of the old stories. There will be no more treachery through the written word.

Last year, despite my best administrations, there was famine in the land. The people said it was because I had committed sacrilegious acts and offended the gods. They dared to rise against me and came to the very walls of Agade. I sallied forth at the head of my troops and destroyed the rebels. The people are ungrateful and foolish: they know nothing of the challenges of kingship. I am growing old now. I have ruled this land for over fifty years. When I die, the provinces may think to revolt again. I am not afraid for my blood has the blessing of the gods. My sons have been raised as kings: they and their sons will govern this land for generations to come.

Whosoever is exalted as king after me, let him rule as I have ruled.

Let him do as I have done.

******

Think about...

Why do you think Sargon wants his story to be known? What does it imply when Sargon says he is of royal blood? What characteristics is he claiming? He says that he was trained as a gardener. What skills and qualities does this work indicate for a future ruler?

Sargon can interpret the meaning of dreams. In those days dreams were seen as indications of the future. Does Sargon use his power for good or ill? Why do you think he acts as he does? Do you think his behaviour is justified?

What do you think dreams really mean? Are they messages from our unconscious, or missives from the gods, or simply a spring-cleaning of the psyche? To what extent do actions make dreams come true?

Can you think of any other stories where dreams are significant?

Can you think of any modern parallels to this story?

Task

Everything that you do starts off as an idea in our mind. From a cup of coffee to an international business, you have to imagine it before you can make it happen. The difference between dreams and reality is often simply a matter of action. You can work to make your own dreams come true. The trick is simply to stop sabotaging yourself.

What would you really like to do? Try to think of at least five things. This can include anything you want, however crazy it might seem. You can always change your ideas later.

Make a list of things you dream about:
1. Learn to play the guitar
2. Visit my friend in Australia
3. Play tennis regularly
4. Have a painting in an exhibition
5. Re-train as a football coach....

Now set a specific objective beside each item:
1. Ask at the music shop about teachers
2. Look on the internet for flights
3. Book a court at the sports club
4. Contact a small local art gallery
5. Find out about training courses....

Put a date beside each task and make a note in your diary. As you complete each objective, make a similar note for the next step. If one of your dreams turns out to be unrealistic right now, how could you modify it so that it becomes attainable? Be prepared to accept a substitute or reasonable compromise. You can't be a surf instructor if you live in the mountains: could you move, or teach climbing instead? The partner of your dreams may already be committed: how might you meet someone with similar characteristics? What would this involve? What will you do next?

For example,

.....

2. Find out about working holidays in Australia

.....

5. Volunteer to coach the local junior football team

.....

Even Mount Everest can only be climbed one step at a time. By breaking things down into small manageable tasks, we will find that we can achieve more than we ever imagined.

8. The Urchin

The Urchin is another manifestation of the child archetype. Unlike his counterpart, he is not born with a silver spoon in his mouth. Whereas the Prince is privileged by virtue of his blood (or in the case of the Foundling, attains what is only his natural birthright), the Urchin has to survive on nothing but his natural wits and luck. He is the alter ego of the Prince: lowly in stature and outwardly unprepossessing, he must gain by guile what the Prince was freely given. The Urchin usually wins, but he does so against the odds. We identify with both these archetypes because they reflect different aspects of experienced reality. As children we each feel special but the world inexplicably fails to recognize this, forcing us to fend for ourselves.

The figure of the Urchin abounds in folktale, where the poor boy makes good through a combination of wit, luck and favours acquired by good-natured deeds. This character is defined by financial circumstances rather than family background. His status is determined by the lack of material possessions rather than by breeding. He may be of noble blood, but if so has older siblings whose claims take precedence. The Urchin is often a third or seventh son, so will not gain anything through inheritance. Instead he must leave home to seek his fortune elsewhere. He is often slightly simple, although usually good-natured. Jack meets his Giant after credulously exchanging the family cow for a handful of beans. Hansel drops breadcrumbs to mark the way home, and the birds eat them. Celtic Niall gives the hag at the well a kiss in exchange for a bucket of water; it is a bonus when she transmutes into a beautiful woman. Russian Ivan loses his arrow in the swamp; he finds a frog-wife who manages to complete the tasks necessary to win the tsar's throne.

Small children often identify strongly with this archetype. Never able to compete with their older brothers and sisters, they draw comfort from stories where the youngest member of the family ultimately does best. Real life often follows the same pattern, as birth order affects our family roles. The eldest child is typically serious and hard-working, bearing the burden of parental hopes and dreams. Younger siblings are relieved of this responsibility and are consequently carefree: creative characters are often ultimately more successful in life.

The Urchin may be poor in material assets but he is usually content with his lot. Naturally optimistic, he is good company and consequently finds friends wherever he goes. Unlike Oliver, the Artful Dodger does not have a long-lost wealthy grandfather, but nor would he want one: he and Fagin are engaged in a mutually satisfactory working relationship. The Urchin may win the hand of a princess, but he will be equally happy with a good-natured barmaid. However, he can be remarkably cunning in getting what he wants. The infant Hermes steals the cattle of Apollo, Greek god of the Sun, and drives them backwards so that their hoof-prints will not give him away. Maori Maui tells his big brothers how to catch the sun, slowing it down so that the day is long enough for both work and play. Huckleberry Finn is full of stratagems to help him along the way. In fact the Urchin often grows up to be the Trickster, continuing his antics in adult life.

The boy in the following story is not rich but nor is he easily demoralized. He may be ragged but he is resourceful and persevering. When at first he fails in his quest, he determines to try again. In life what matters is not how we greet success but how we respond to failure. It is only when we get up and brush off the dirt that we have another chance. The Urchin sees his mistakes as an opportunity to learn. This willingness to keep trying reminds us that he is still a child. As toddlers we have to get up after every tumble, or we would never learn to walk: only in later life do we learn to interpret setbacks as final. We find the Urchin endearing because his persistence shows an innocence of spirit. Despite all his ruses, he is still somehow ingenious. He is happy to share whatever fortune brings him. His good nature ensures that he will be accepted wherever he goes. When he makes his final choice, we have no doubt that it will be the right one.[1]

The Worn-Out Shoes

(A German Folktale)

One day a boy came walking over the hill above the town. He had left home full of dreams, hoping to see the world; but dreams do not fill your stomach, and now he had nothing left but a little bread and cheese in his bundle. Still, the view was a fine one and he sat down to eat his lunch. An old woman came up behind him and spoke:

"Can you spare me a little food, young sir?"

"Gladly, grandmother," he replied. "But you'll have to share what you see, for I've nothing else."

"In that case, I'll tell you something in exchange," she said. "Down there lives a king with twelve beautiful daughters. Every night they disappear, and no-one can tell where they go. The doors are locked, but in the morning their fine shoes are quite worn-out. The king has promised that anyone who can discover their secret may marry one of them, and have a share of the kingdom. My advice to you is this: do not take what you are offered until you have the answer to this puzzle."

The boy looked down at his own old shoes and laughed.

"Truly, it would be a fine thing to marry a princess and rule my own land."

But when he turned around to thank the old woman, she had disappeared.

The boy made his way down into the town and knocked at the gates of the palace. When the king heard what he had come for, he began to laugh: princes had tried and failed to find where his daughters went, and here was a ragged peasant boy wanting to try his luck. Nonetheless, the eldest princess treated him as courteously as she would any suitor. She led him to a small room which led off the girls' bedchamber. There, she filled a tub with hot water, and threw in a handful of cleansing herbs. She helped him to remove his ragged shirt and trousers. Then she withdrew, leaving him alone.

The boy longed to climb into the bath and soak the dust from his feet, but he feared that he would be lulled to sleep by the scent of the herbs. He pressed his shirt against his face to keep out the fumes and stole to the curtain. He was just in time to see the last princess disappearing through a hole in the floor. She lowered the trapdoor behind her and there was nothing to show where she had gone. The boy kept his eyes on the spot and felt along the floor with his fingers until he found the edge of the flap. He managed to prise it open with his pocket-knife, and lay there silently as the sound of voices receded into the distance. Then he swung his feet down into the darkness, and felt a ladder fastened against the wall. He clambered down and found himself alone in a forest. There was no sign of the girls, and no tracks to indicate which way they had gone. The boy felt foolish, but determined that they would not escape him so easily again. He broke off a branch from a tree as evidence of his visit, then climbed back up the ladder. It had been a long day, and the smell of the herbs was overpowering. By the time the princesses returned, he was already fast asleep.

The boy woke refreshed and spent the day in his room, wondering how he could contrive to follow the girls. He sent word to the king that he had rested, and was ready to start his quest. That night, the eldest princess led him to the anteroom and brought him a tray of food which she had cooked herself. The boy was about to eat when he remembered the old woman's advice. After a minute he stole to the curtain and saw the youngest princess climbing down through the trapdoor. He slipped across the room and managed to catch the flap as it fell. He slid down the ladder quickly, and followed close behind the girls. The youngest princess walked last, and seemed to sense his presence: several times she turned around and peered through the trees, but the boy kept very still and she did not see him.

Once her hair ribbon caught on a twig, and when the boy came past he pulled it off and put it in his pocket. The girls came to the edge of a lake, where a great boat shaped like a swan was waiting for them. They climbed into the boat and it rowed away towards a grand palace filled with lights and music. Discouraged, the boy turned around and made his way back to the ladder. Back in his room, he started to eat his supper but he soon began to feel drowsy. When the eldest princess peered in later, he was deeply asleep.

The next morning, the boy did not seem discouraged. In fact, he asked the king for one final chance. The eldest daughter agreed, but this time she was taking no chances. As the boy lay in his room that evening, she brought him a cup of hot wine laced with spices. She knelt beside the bed and watched him as he drank. The boy remembered the old woman's warning and let the hot liquid dribble down his neck. It was hot and sticky under his collar but he thanked her politely. Smiling graciously, the princess rose and took the cup. She turned in the doorway to look back: the boy closed his eyes and began to snore. Satisfied, she let the curtain fall into place. At once the boy leapt to his feet and ran across the room. The princesses were already gone, but this time the trapdoor had been left ajar. The boy climbed silently down, and followed them through the woods. When they came to the lake, the boy hid his clothes behind a tree and swam out after them. In the great hall, musicians played and a thousand candles shone. The twelve princesses were greeted by twelve handsome lords. They started to dance, all except the youngest who still seemed worried. She sat in a window seat watching her sisters. The boy crept up beneath the window, and reaching in he took the bronze cup from which she had been drinking. When she found it was gone she turned round with a cry, but he had already disappeared. The boy swam back across the lake, pulled on his clothes and hurried home through the forest. When the eldest princess peeked in through the curtain, he grinned at her.

Next morning, the king summoned him to give an account of his findings and the boy told him all that he had seen. He produced the branch in evidence, then the hair ribbon, and finally the bronze cup. The king examined them thoughtfully and turned to his daughters.

"Well, my dears, you have heard this boy's report. Is this true?"

The youngest princess tugged at her hair ribbon and began to cry. The eldest princess looked hard at the boy, and then she turned to the king.

"Yes, father, he has discovered our secret. What he says is all true."

"In that case he can marry one of you and have a share of the kingdom, as I promised."

The boy looked at the line of girls. The eldest princess stared back at him. The youngest wiped her eyes and sniffed. The others were all scowling at the ground.

And he made his choice.

****

Think about...

When and where is this story set? How might it be different in another time or place? Could it happen to a poor boy today?

Have you ever met anyone like the boy in this story? In what ways were they similar? What was your relationship with them?

Think of a time when you had to rely on your wits. What was the situation? Where did this happen? Who else was involved? What did you do?

What other archetypal figures can you identify in this story? What is their relationship to the main figure? What does each one contribute to the plot development?

Whom did the boy choose? Will they be happy together?

Task

Has life turned out as you though it would? How do you feel about your life now? What are you happy about, or pleased to have achieved? What would you do differently if you had another chance?

Sometimes you may look back and wonder why you made certain choices. Do not judge your younger self too harshly, but try to remember how the world looked to you back then. Remind yourself that you did not know then what you do now. Have confidence that your younger self acted in good faith. Your 'inner child' is a part of who you are today: your childhood dreams still influence you more than you are aware.

What was your favourite fairy tale as a child? Why did this story appeal to you?

Imagine that you could act out this story with yourself in the starring role! Write down the names of the main characters, then decide:

i) Who would you choose to play these parts? Cast characters from your real world to act these roles. You can mix past and present, bringing together people from different parts of your life.

ii) What happens in your story? Where will you set the action? Are there any extra details you would like to add? An extra character or an explanatory scene?

iii) How will your story end? Think about what might happen afterwards.

Write your story out in full. You can have a lot of fun playing with the characters and events. And remember that you can choose what will happen next!

9. The Hero

The hero is the quintessential adult male. He is perhaps the most popular of the archetypes, appearing in stories from every time and place. We recognize him by his good looks and toned physique. Instinctively we know that his chiselled profile is accompanied by a fine sense of social responsibility. Excelling both physically and morally, the hero has an energy that exceeds normal human strength. His character and capacity for action mark him out as an example of *arête*, excellence. The hero has no doubts about his own abilities: he walks with a certain swagger in his step. From the moment we meet him, we feel that things are going to be different around here.

Although he exhibits almost supernatural powers, the hero is a man and not a god. Sometimes he is ascribed divine paternity but the hero is always fully human. His achievements provide us with an example which we can aspire to. In excelling the normal bounds of mortality, the hero becomes a vision of potential for his people. The hero incarnates man in his most noble aspect. His greatest threat comes not from outside, but from within himself. His natural virility is accompanied by a tendency to excessive violence. At times the behaviour of the hero risks transgressing normal social boundaries. To qualify for the title, the hero must use force without being overcome by his own aggression.[1]

The way that we perceive heroes has altered over the centuries. In pre-historic times people relied on the bravery of male hunters to provide protein for a balanced diet. The virility and violence of the hero were revered because they were vital for the survival of the tribe. The poor judgement shown by many teenage boys reflects the value once ascribed to acts of inordinate bravery during the hunt. This high esteem persisted into the Bronze Age and the advent of warrior societies. Achilles is lauded by Homer in the *Iliad* despite his uncontrollable rage over the death of his friend Patroclus. The Irish champion CuChulainn frequently goes looking for trouble; at one point he is only checked by embarrassment at the approach of numerous naked women. A similar tactic is used to quell the wrath of the Greek hero Bellerophon when he returns from his trials.

With the development of agricultural techniques, social values began to shift. Settled agrarian communities no longer relied on the bursts of action required for a hunt. Heroes were now required to have brains as well as brawn. The knight is a champion who must also exhibit chivalry, honour and romance. This is even more true of our technological lifestyle today. Weapons of long-distance destruction render arduous physical training obsolete. This has created a crisis of identity for young males in our society. In the absence of acceptable role models, they are forced to develop their own definitions and tests of masculinity. Their images are often constrained by limited peer-group resources. The huge popularity of quest-based computer games attests to the enduring need for heroic goals. Tales of warrior knights remain close to the original essence of the hero archetype.[2]

Modern definitions of the hero show that we now value very different characteristics. As civilizations become more sophisticated, the rewards for taking extreme risks decrease. Modern heroes reflect a shift in values as mental agility has replaced the need for physical strength. The saint and the saviour-sage are later variants of the hero image. Figures like Gandhi, Mandela and Martin Luther promoted social revolution by non-violent means. There is still a place for men of action in modern times, and individual acts of bravery are praised and prized. Clint Eastwood's generic character reminds us that a hard man is good to find. Sports stars are paid huge sums of money for their achievements. On the whole, however, we like our idols to have brains as well as biceps. Indiana Jones shows us that a thinking man can handle a bullwhip. James Bond combines physical

prowess with astute analysis and devastating charm. The difficulty for the modern hero is reconciling his rampant virility with
his sensitive side. He is expected to have feelings but he must
never show fear. We like our protectors to be pillars of strength,
swallowing emotion for the greater good. Humphrey Bogart in
Casablanca is an anti-hero, studiedly cynical but sacrificing his
personal happiness for a higher cause. He receives no acclaim for
his actions, but the adoring audience know what he has given
up.

The myths of Ancient Greece present the prototypical model
of the hero. These paragons were usually born of a mortal
woman and a god: they were thus set above common humanity.
Many Greek cities claimed such a semi-divine protagonist as
their founder or protector. They were not deities, but heroes such
as Herakles could gain immortality through their actions. Their
stories are not unequivocally happy ones: frequently the hero
has to plumb the depths of despair before he can overcome his
adversary. In many cases his subsequent behaviour leads to loss
or even exile. Bellerophon's behaviour transgressed the bounds
of society and hospitality. In punishment, he is sent on an almost
impossible mission to destroy the fire-breathing Chimaera.
These stories show us both how, and how not, to behave. In
transgressing the normal bounds of human conduct, the hero
both challenges and reaffirms the values and beliefs of society.

Bel and the Chimaera

(A Greek Myth)

Characters in order of appearance:

Bel, a young nobleman
Aethra, Bel's girlfriend
Russell, Aethra's cousin
Deliades, Bel's brother
Proetus, a rich man of Tiryns
Anteia, the young wife of Proetus
Iobates, head of Lycian Metals Inc.
Athene, a Greek goddess
Philonoe, daughter of Iobates

Act I

Scene 1: An alley in Corinth lit by a single street-lamp. Bel stands looking up at a window. Aethra is pulling petals from the flowers in a window box and dropping them on him like confetti.

Bel: Stay, sweetheart; your father will surely be working late again tonight.

Aethra: He is so busy. I would be lonesome here if it were not for you.

Bel: I hope his business will keep him in Corinth longer, if you stay too.

Aethra: Has your father spoken to mine yet?

Bel: Only in private; but I think the match will be advantageous to them both.

Aethra (jokingly): What arrogance! You are so certain he will approve of you?

Bel: For sure! My good breeding is shown in the excellence of my choice.

Aethra: I will not talk longer. Someone is coming and I should not be seen.

(She ducks inside the window and closes the shutters as a man runs up).

Russell: Hey, fellow! What are you doing there?

Bel: Why should you care if I choose to stand here?

Russell: The house is dark: you can have no honest business.

Bel: Indeed. Since you have come, I will now go.

Russell: As I thought! You planned to rob the place! Stop thief!

(He reaches into his jacket. Bel pulls out a knife and lunges first. Russell falls to the ground.)

Bel: That will teach you to mind your own business, whoever you are.

(He wipes his blade on the prostrate body. Enter Deliades.)

Bel: Hey, big brother. Just in time to save me again... or not.

(He kicks the body over and the lamp illuminates his face).

Deliades: What have you done? Oh gods... Do you not recognize him? It is the nephew of this house, your girl Aethra's cousin.

Bel: Heaven forgive me. I thought only to defend myself. What shall I do?

Deliades: Our father cannot let this pass. Too much rests upon the treaty negotiations.

Bel: Then there is no hope for me. My love and my life are both forfeit from this act.

Deliades: You must leave this town tonight. I will give you what means I can. Fare well!

Act II

Scene 1: The main room of Proetus' house in Tiryns. Proetus and Bel enter, slightly the worse for drink.

Bel: You are a fine friend for one so newly met!

Proetus: It was the Fates who brought us both to the same bar

99

tonight.

Bel: It is good of you to let me stay here.

Proetus: Say nothing of it. My wife will enjoy the company when I am out.

Bel: Tomorrow I will start to look for work.

Proetus: Best you get an early night then. There are blankets on the couch.

(He rises and ambles from the room. A moment later, his wife Anteia enters).

Anteia: I heard we have a guest. My husband is most hospitable.

Bel: I am sorry to trouble you. I am newly come to Tiryns.

(Anteia looks him up and down, then moves suggestively closer).

Anteia: It is no trouble. Is everything to your satisfaction?

Bel: Yes, thank you. I have everything I need.

Anteia: But perhaps this would make you more comfortable?

(She wraps her arms around his neck. Bel hesitates for a moment, then responds with growing enthusiasm. Proetus returns and peers short-sightedly at them.)

Proetus: I forgot my spectacles. Is everything alright?

Bel: I don't... I mean... I need the bathroom.

(Exit Bel hurriedly, clutching his trousers.)

Anteia: That insolent brat! Thank goodness you came back.

Proetus: What has he done? You are shaking, my love. Did he hurt you?

Anteia: I managed to fend him off. Let us not speak of it again, my dear.

Proetus: I am sorry that I brought him here. He must leave in the morning. You will not have to face him again.

(He embraces his wife and thinks for a moment).

Proetus: I will find a pretext to get rid of him. I'll send him to your father with a letter explaining the circumstances. Perhaps he can find him some work out in the provinces.

Scene 2: The office of Iobates, head of Lycian Metals Inc.

Iobates: This letter says you need a job. But you come with neither record nor references. Tell me, what can you do?

Bel: I can read and write, ride a horse and handle a sword well.

Iobates: Fine skills no doubt, but not of much use to an employer.

Bel: Give me the chance to prove myself and you will see my worth.

Iobates: Pride is of little value until proven. A beggar cannot state his price.

Bel: (Scowling) I will try anything. You will not regret your kind consideration.

Iobates: Very well. We will see what you are made of.

(Pauses, considering; then slowly smiles).

I will send you to the Chimaera Mines with a note of commendation.

Act III

Scene 1: Entrance to the Chimaera Mines. The goddess Athene, dressed as a works supervisor, addresses the audience directly.

Athene: My favourite has shown himself a true hero. I will show you what has passed here.

(Voices off cry: "Fire!" "Help!" Bel emerges from the tunnel entrance. His clothes are torn and dirty. He wipes his brow and stares at the goddess in some confusion).

Athene: Greetings, Bel. Tell us what has happened.

Bel: We were blasting a new vein. There must have been gas in the tunnel: a spark set it alight. The timbers are all ablaze. The shaft will collapse and the mine will be finished.

Athene: Think now. What must be done?

Bel: We must contain the fire. If only we could seal the side tunnel....

Athene: This trolley is loaded with metal ingots. Will you dare the blaze?

Bel: Have I the courage and the strength? Give me the harness!

(He hauls the trolley into the mine entrance and disappears from sight. Terrible clashing and hissing noises. Athene clasps her hands and gazes upwards. At last Bel re-appears.)

Bel: It is done. The wall is made. The heat from the fire will seal it.

Athene: The mine is saved. You have done a great thing indeed. Truly you are a champion like the monster-slayers of old. Your behaviour and my report will surely recommend you to Iobates now.

(Exhausted, Bel collapses unconscious as the lights fade.)

Scene 2: The office of Iobates at Lycian Metals Inc.

Iobates: I hear that you have acquitted yourself well. Thanks to you, our interests are safe.

Bel: Now your trust is repaid. My deeds will stand as my record and reference.

Iobates: Your curriculum vita looks extremely interesting. I hope that you will stay with the company. There is a position involving trade and negotiation which I believe would suit you very well. The prospects are exceedingly good.

(Enter Philonoe, carrying a pile of papers. She smiles coyly at Bel.)

Iobates: Have you met my younger daughter? She works in the accounts department.

Bel: Thank you, sir. I would be delighted to accept the job.

****

Think about...

For each Act: Why do you think Bel behaves as he does? What does he achieve by this behaviour? Who is affected by his actions? Do you feel that his conduct is justified?

When and where do you think this story takes place? What clues provide this context? How does the setting affect what happens? What other play, myths or stories does this remind you of? How do these parallels affect your interpretation of the plot?

Can you think of any modern parallels to this story? How do heroes behave today?

Is Bel born a hero, or does he become one? Which makes us heroic, our intentions or our actions?

Does Bel remind you of anyone you have met? How well do you know this person? What is your opinion of them?

Task

The hero risks everything to complete his mission. We may admire him, but his position is often hard to understand. What motivates him to act in this way?

Think of a hero whom you would like to know better. This could be a fictional character from a book or film, or a real-life person whom you have heard of in the press. Imagine you are going to interview this person. Prepare for the meeting carefully. You will need pencils and paper. If possible, find a picture of your subject. Note down what you already know about this person. Write down the questions that you are going to ask.

Now you are ready to conduct the interview. It may be helpful to set up two chairs for the session: one is yours, the other is for your interviewee. Greet the person and ask your first question. Then move, either mentally or physically, to their position. Become that other person: think as they think, see the world through their eyes. As this person, give your answer to the question. Now come back to your original place and note the answer down. Repeat this process with the other questions. At the end, thank your subject and say goodbye.

Write up your interview in the form of a newspaper article. How has your understanding of the subject increased? What lessons have you learned that you could apply in your own life?

10. The Trickster

Tales of tricks and pranks appeal to everyone. We all like a good laugh, so long as the joke is not on us. The Trickster is an archetypal figure who manifests in myths and legends from around the world. He appeals to the anarchist in all of us. He is a clown and a natural rebel. He does the things that we would like to do, if we were not afraid of the consequences. Some of the best stories are those with a 'twist in the tail': the geek gets the girl; the little kid wreaks revenge on the class bully. It is gratifying to hear that the proud and privileged will not always have things their own way. We identify with the small figure who manages to win against all the odds. If we cannot attain our ends by force, we can always resort to low cunning. The Trickster breaks social taboos, although the results of his behaviour ultimately reinforce them. He is greedy, lustful and pathologically selfish. In spite of this, good often comes of his actions.

In Native American stories the trickster is most often Coyote. In different areas other animals – Rabbit or Raven – also play pranks, but Old Man Coyote often appears in the stories as their comrade and fellow mischief-maker. Trickster tales are told to amuse as much as to edify. Coyote is a buffoon who usually gets his come-uppance in the end. His story is a warning of the pitfalls of trying to cheat or steal from others in the community. Yet Coyote is painfully human in his imperfections. Even when his plans backfire, he always manages to arouse our sympathy and amusement. On occasion he is even a culture-hero, as when he steals fire from the gods for mankind. Different Tricksters appear in other parts of the world but their stories are similar. Across West Africa, the spider-god Anansi is proverbial for his cunning. In Nigeria, the trickster is Tortoise; in eastern and southern Africa, he is Hare. When black slaves were taken from Africa to work the plantations of America, they blended traditional lore with local traditions and told the adventures of a new trickster-hero, Brer Rabbit.[1]

The figure of the trickster is the shadowy counterpart of the glorious hero. Each of them needs the other to give meaning to their existence. The Joker acknowledges Batman as his only worthy adversary. Iago's position is defined by his jealousy of Othello. Sometimes the two figures merge into a single ambivalent character. Jack Kerouac glorifies in his status of outsider 'on the road'. The Great Gatsby is ultimately unmasked but we do not have the heart to condemn his actions. Toad of Toad Hall is a menace to his friends but they remain loyal to him. Although the Trickster may deserve his downfall, we feel empathy for him as well as amusement.

The Trickster possesses a fundamental wisdom born of his position as an outsider. The Jester uses humour to mask unpalatable insights: only the Fool dares speak truthfully to the King. Sometimes the Trickster is dangerous, for knowledge confers power which can be misused. A more malevolent manifestation of this archetype is the Devil, the figure standing in some sacred stories against the main creator. We project malign motives onto this character partly because we do not fully understand him. Our word 'devil' derives from the Indian word *deva* or deity: the gods of one religion become the demons of another. Lucifer, the devil of Christian scriptures, was originally the angel who loved God most. He refused to divert honour to God's creation, and for this insubordination was cast out of heaven. The figure of the devil conjures up our distrust of the unknown. If we can discard our prejudices, we will find that this character has much to teach us.[2]

Trickster tales are a potent metaphor for the capricious nature of existence. Some children are born with the proverbial silver spoon in their mouth. The Trickster has to face the world armed only with the power of his own wits. Confronted by powerful obstacles or adversaries, the Trickster must rely on his own cunning for survival. Although he is sly and selfish, we sympathize with his dilemmas. The trickster is Everyman, a flawed figure with whom we can all at times identify. Although at times defeated, he is never totally destroyed. Indeed his actions often turn out for the general good. The Trickster is a cosmic clown: even in adversity, he generates laughter. Through the humour inherent in the stories, we are given the courage to face and hopefully transcend our own problems. The Trickster may suffer the consequences of his actions, but he always relishes life to the full. Never quite overcome, he gives eternal hope to the common man in his daily struggles.[3]

One of the great figures of Scandinavian mythology is Loki the Trickster. The tales of the Norsemen reflect Viking values: bravery and honour, loyalty and hospitality. The bright gods of Asgard are led by wise Odin; Thor, the god of thunder, is immensely strong; Frey controls agricultural fertility. The gods represent culture and order, although they are impetuous and their morality is sometimes questionable. They are in constant conflict with the ice giants, who embody the cold northern winters. Metaphorically, the gods defend the achievements of human civilization against the chaotic forces of nature which constantly threaten to overwhelm them. Loki is an outsider, an ambivalent figure who provides the gods with their greatest treasures yet ultimately plots their downfall. Tales of the Trickster remind us of the fickleness of life in this harsh world.

Loki of the Crooked Mouth

(A Norse Myth)

Try to see it my way. There I was, minding my own business, when she winked at me. I'm a married man but you must understand it was tempting. Not that I'd ever hurt my wife – she thinks the world of me – but this had nothing to do with her. Sif caught my eye across the room and tossed her blonde hair over her shoulder. You can see why she was interested. Her husband's a brute of a man with a big bushy beard, not the brightest of fellows. I imagine that Sif just fancied a piece of the other, something a bit exotic for a change. She threw me her dazzling smile and I followed her like a shadow. We slipped out of the hall and made our way to her chamber. Afterwards she fell asleep, and I leaned on one elbow looking down at her. She really was extraordinarily beautiful. Even I could hardly credit my luck, and the lads would certainly never believe it. I curled a lock of that corn-gold hair around my finger. It occurred to me that it would make a fond souvenir.

That was where the trouble started. Thor heard I had the hair, and he hauled me in front of the council. Believe me, I thought they were going to lynch me. I couldn't betray Sif – that would be discourteous, and besides they would never take my word against hers. I had to think fast, and the story had to be a good one.

"I admit, it's Sif's hair," I said. "I cut it as she slept. She knew nothing about it."

I could see her from the corner of my eye, but she would not look at me.

"So how did you come to be in my wife's bed-chamber?" Thor thundered. "How did you get through a locked door?"

"I flew in through the keyhole. I... I took the form of a fly."

Surely that would stretch even Thor's credulity, but there is no limit to what people will believe. The claim that a foreigner could turn into a fly was more palatable than the thought that his wife might have willingly opened her room to me. He half-turned to face the assembled throng.

"Then I demand that you restore Sif's hair."

This was asking the impossible, but I was in no position to object? After all, I could turn into an insect and pass through a keyhole. And the alternative was either death or banishment. Shakily I nodded, and Thor released my collar so abruptly that I nearly fell. The crowd had already lost interest in me; the thrum of conversation covered my retreat. Keeping my head down, I slunk out of the great hall.

I left at once, for my face was clearly not welcome in Asgard right now. I crossed the rainbow bridge and made my way to Svartalfheim, home of the dwarves. I'd been there before on business, and I knew my way around. They make some lovely pieces which would be just the thing for my current predicament. I found Dvalin, who is the best craftsman of them all. I told him that I wanted a hair-piece for my girl: it pleased me that I could give her a love-gift right under her husband's nose. He made me a clip hung with fine strings of pure gold. I thought that I could get on the right side of the gods while I was at it, so I found presents for them too. There was a great spear - just the thing for Odin, who likes to throw his weight around. For Frey there was a golden ship which could be folded up to fit in your pocket: a gimmick, but it might come in useful for long journeys. I was well pleased, and I told Dvalin so. It pays to keep dealings sweet with these artistic types.

"Good work, mate," I said. "No-one makes stuff to beat yours, and that's a fact."

It was bad luck that Brok was passing, because there's always been trouble between those two.

"My brother Sindri's a far better smith than Dvalin," he yelled. "I'll wager my head on it."

Now, I saw a chance to get something for nothing so I came back to him fast.

"You're on," I said. "Three things to match these, or you'll owe me serious stakes."

Well, Brok took the bait like a dream. He rushed off to his brother and told him of the bet. Sindri mixed his metals and fired up the furnace, then he went to work. He made a golden boar for Frey, but it was the sort of trinket you'd give to a lady so I felt quite safe. He fashioned a gold arm-band for Odin, but it looked a bit flash for a bloke in his position. Last of all he fetched an iron bar and set it to heat in the flames. When it was red-hot he drew it out and began to beat it into shape. All this time Brok had been pumping the bellows, and by now he looked almost beat himself. A drop of sweat slid down his forehead, shining in the firelight like a beetle. He paused to brush it away and gave me a nasty grin. Sindri saw him stop and gave him a piece of his mind, and he almost spoiled the job as a result. It turned out to be a hammer, a little short in the handle but a fine piece of work nonetheless. My heart sank when I saw it, for I knew at once that Thor would like it. Toys for the boys, that's the way to appeal to him.

The dwarves came back to Asgard with me, to hear the judgement of the gods. Odin, Frey and Thor sat at one side of the big table; the other gods stood ranged in groups along the walls. We gave them Dvalin's gifts first. Thor took the hair-piece and fastened it solemnly in Sif's hair: she was obviously trying not to laugh at the great oaf. He seemed to feel that honour had been satisfied, and I breathed a sigh of relief. Odin wanted to go outside at once and try his new spear. Frey seemed quite pleased with the ship, and slipped it into his pocket to examine later. Then it was Brok's turn. Frey obviously wasn't over-impressed with the boar pendant. Odin took his arm-ring and handed it to one of the servants for safekeeping: jewellery patently wasn't his thing. But Thor seized the hammer with a shout of joy and I knew I was in trouble. He hadn't exactly been on my side in the first place, and now I was clearly history.

"This has got to be the winner," he exclaimed. "With a weapon like this, I could eliminate the ice giants!"

He had obviously forgotten that I was not the only one in the room with foreign blood.

There was a long moment of silence. Then Brok spoke, his voice smooth with subservience and malice.

"So it seems that I am the winner," he said. "Before the gods, I come to claim my prize. By the terms of our wager, Loki's head is mine."

I backed up the room looking around for help, but no-one wanted to catch my eye. Don't lie with a man when he's down, they say: you're liable to get trodden on too. A draught from the door licked the back of my neck with chill promise. I turned and made a run for it.

Brok screeched with wrath and Thor was after me at once. With that weight you'd think he was a slow runner, but he puts on a good turn of speed over short distances. I stumbled and he dropped on me like a thunderbolt. He dragged me back to the great hall where the gods waited in silence to witness my demise.

As Thor stomped up the room with my hair in his fist I was thinking fast. When he put me down I turned to Odin, appealing to him as the greatest of the gods.

"If you judge Brok's gifts to be the best, then so it must be. Allfather, consider these tributes to your glory. What do you decide?"

Odin sighed slowly. I do not think at that moment he truly hated me. Nonetheless, his judgement had to be in line with popular opinion. How else can a ruler maintain his power?

"With this hammer, Thor can keep the ice giants at bay. The gods will be safe in Asgard until the end of this world. It is truly a wonderful thing."

Brok the Dwarf stepped forwards, his face twisted with

anticipation.

"Odin agrees that Loki's head is forfeit. That should stop his troublemaking."

Thor was smirking in the background. We had been friends once: supped together, travelled together. Those times were obviously forgotten. None of the other gods spoke up in my support.

"I submit to your judgement, great one," I said. The words stuck in my throat, but they were necessary to oil his pride. "But hear this: Brok has no claim upon my neck. If he can find a way to remove my head without hurting my neck, then he may take his prize."

Odin slapped his hand on his thigh and gave a great bellow of laughter. The other gods stood silent until his mirth had subsided. Then he leaned forwards and looked at me seriously.

"You are always a slippery one, my Loki," he said. "Truth to tell, I don't know what we would do without you to lighten our long winter evenings. Your point is a fair one. Brok may take your head, but in so doing he must not harm a single hair on your neck."

Brok was seething, but he knew that he was beaten. Still he would not leave without some gesture of his spite.

"Very well, very well. But grant that I can treat my property as I like. I will not take the head with me, for that would entail Loki's company which I can well do without. But I will silence his boasting and his insults. Yes, I will seal his lips before I go."

And so he sewed my mouth shut. Thor held me fast whilst the dwarf picked out his awl. He drove it through my lips: first the upper, then the lower. He threaded a leather thong through the holes like a shoemaker lacing a boot. It did not really hurt, no more than the knife-prick when you swear blood-kinship with a new brother. Certainly not enough to let them see me flinch. The crowd laughed at my discomfort, but when I showed no pain they lost interest and turned away. Sif sat at the far end of the hall: her face was pale, but she spoke no word to stop the circus. The dwarf knotted the thread and grinned maliciously, but my eyes were far away. Thor loosened his grip and looked at me uncertainly. I would not give him the satisfaction of acknowledgment. That great clown had no idea of the harm he had done. My people are quick to please, but we have our pride. Let it fester until the world's end, I will never forgive an insult.

My loyal wife drew out the thong and bathed my lips in saltwater. They healed soon enough, but the laceration left a scar. After that day my smile was always crooked. And there was a hard dark tumour in my heart.

The bright gods were fools that day in Asgard.

Stupid. Stupid. Stupid.

******

Think about...

Who precipitates the action in this story? What do you think of Loki's behaviour? Are Thor's reactions justified? How do you feel about Sif's role?

Do you think that Loki is clever, or too smart for his own good? What causes him to act in this way? Is he innately bad, or are his motivations more complex? Who benefits or suffers from his actions? Does he deserve to be punished for his trickery?

What other stories does this remind you of? Do you know any other trickster figures from different traditions?

Have you ever been involved in a similar situation? What happened? How did you feel about it? What did you do?

What other archetypal figures can you identify in this myth? How can you recognize them, by their appearance or their behaviour?

Which character do you sympathize with most, and why?

Task

The Trickster faces the world armed only with the power of his own wits. No matter how safe you try to make your life, there will be times when you are thrown back on your own resources. Sometimes the threat will be external - a drunk on the street or a thief in the night; sometimes it will be something more invidious — a mischievous rumour or hurtful comment. If you respond correctly to these situations, there is a good chance that everything will be all right.

You have been conditioned to act in socially acceptable ways. It can be hard to override patterns of polite behaviour and react spontaneously in difficult situations. You must learn to trust your instincts in order to keep yourself safe. One way of doing this is to identify with an appropriate archetype. By imaging an appropriate role model, you allow your subconscious minds to respond spontaneously and appropriately to circumstances. You can draw on the power of the trickster to react creatively in your own life.

Think of a 'tricky' situation that you have faced recently, or are currently experiencing. Perhaps you had a quarrel with a neighbour; or a friend has betrayed your confidence; or someone's actions have put you in a difficult position.... Rather than confront the troublemaker directly, perhaps you could approach the problem in another way. How could you use the power of the trickster? Could you put the perpetrator in a similar position or somehow instigate a truce? Try to use humour and the principle of 'like-for-like'. Think about consequences rather than confrontation. Perhaps you could talk about it with a friend: whatever you feel inside, try to keep the mood light-hearted.

Brainstorm all the solutions you can think of, and write them all down. Be as creative as you can, and don't be afraid to be whacky. Then choose the one that you think has the best chance of success. And if at first you don't succeed, remember that the Trickster never gives up: there is always another time....

11. The Wise Man

Every hero needs a mentor as he sets out on his quest. When the wise man appears, we know that his advice will be good. We recognize him at once despite the hat pulled down to hide his face. He wears a heavy cloak and carries a wooden staff. His silver hair and lined countenance reflect his age and experience. His demeanour evokes instinctive feelings of reassurance and respect. The young adventurer does well to heed the words of this beneficent sage. The wise man who counsels the hero at the start of his journey represents both his ageing father and his own future self.

The figure of the wise man recurs in myths and legends from around the world. In Judao-Christian tradition he is the very image of God. In Norse mythology Odin the Allfather sits on his high seat looking out across the world. Odin has only one eye, having given the other in exchange for a drink from the Well of Knowledge. He wears a blue cloak with a wide-brimmed hat pulled down to hide his missing eye and carries a heavy stick. Gandalf, the magician in *Lord of the Rings*, bears a striking resemblance to Odin because Tolkien admired Norse myths. Celtic tales tell of a wise bard named Taliesin, whom we know by the name of Merlin. It is Merlin who protects the young Arthur and helps him to get the enchanted sword Excalibur. However, even Merlin cannot protect Arthur from his jealous actions in adult life. The wise man can provide advice but we are ultimately responsible for the consequences of our decisions.[1]

For cultures where experience is correlated with knowledge, the wise man is a venerable figure. In traditional societies the elderly are respected as repositories of information and sources of sound advice. Senior officials are usually older men, able to draw upon a wealth of life data when giving judgement and recommendation. The wise man's stature reflects his accumulated life experience. The figure of the bearded sage represents the initiate or priest. In times when fewer people survived to old age, his wisdom was a valuable resource to the community. It is only in the fast-changing world of high technology where information soon becomes obsolete that the elderly are treated as geriatric liabilities. Youth now has the advantage over age, but this is not a permanent state of affairs. In modern society we need physical prowess less than at any other time in human history. Social and economic forces may reinstate the older generation to a position of power and respect.

In Ancient China the image of longevity implied wisdom acquired over many years. In a society where ancestors were worshipped, age was seen as worthy of commensurate respect. From earliest times Chinese scholars have sought the secrets of eternal life. The quest for immortality is also a metaphor for the achievement of spiritual enlightenment. According to Taoist doctrine, the reward of right practice is eternal life. Stories of the Eight Immortals became a central element of popular Taoism. Representing a cross-section of society, these figures confirmed the message that immortality was within the reach of anyone with the right motivation.[2]

The Eight Immortals were immensely popular, with their images appearing on screens, fans and wall scrolls. They are generally shown as a jolly group, relishing the pleasures of eternal life as a reward for their dedication. The first of the group to attain immortality was Li T'ieh-kuai (Li with the Iron Crutch). This ascetic sage was taught knowledge of the Way by the great philosopher Lao Tzu. Li acquired the body of a cripple during the course of his initiation, as is related in the following story. Seeing Li's discomfort, Lao Tzu gave him a crutch on which he could fly through the sky. His other distinguishing emblems are his golden headband and medicinal gourd. Li was later adopted as the patron of pharmacists and his image often adorned their shop signs.

The First Immortal

(A Chinese Legend)

Young men run after many things; they move so fast that opportunities have no chance to introduce themselves. When I was young I decided to devote my life to the attainment of wisdom. This was a great challenge, for the harder you chase insight the more it eludes you. I did not know this then and I spent many years seeking spiritual perfection. When I say this, it is merely to point out the dangers of discouragement. If you persist, then you may undoubtedly succeed in attaining eternal life.

In the end, word of my dedication reached the great sage Lao Tzu and he summoned me to heaven for my final initiation. I prepared at once to heed the summons, taking all due care necessary to ensure my safe return. I left my mortal body on a couch in the garden and instructed my disciple Lang to watch over it. I told him that I would return within seven days: though if I failed to do so he should not mourn, for I would have become pure spirit. Lang was a stupid boy but devoted to me: I knew that he would take his trust with great seriousness. I lay down and closed my eyes; I began to meditate upon the Golden Way. My spirit left my body and soared above the wall, across the fields towards the distant hills. I observed the cowherd at his work, women washing in the river, but none of these worldly things were of concern to me now.

Ah! How to describe the sights and sounds of the immortal realms! Mere words do not suffice: you must study hard and discover these things for yourself. It is for the enlightened to savour, and the unenlightened to aspire. But meanwhile, back on earth time was passing. My visit to Lao was coming to an end. I knew that it was time to go back to my body. Well within the agreed period, my spirit returned to the phenomenal world. Like a bird, my soul skimmed over the mountains and flew across the wide plain. I crossed the river and descended towards the place where I had left my disciple watching over me.

At first I thought that I must have mistaken the spot. Lang was no-where to be seen, and there was no sign of my mortal remains. I looked around for landmarks: everything was where it should be. Could I perchance have returned to the right place but in another time? If so, there was surely no end to my powers now. I stretched myself tall and thin as a length of silk, in the way that only a spirit can stretch. It felt remarkably rejuvenating, but the breeze blowing through me was a little too refreshing. Just then, I caught sight of the cowherd coming down the lane. Either there was a remarkable family likeness, or this was the very man whom I had seen going to his work before I went away. I wafted closer and peered into his face. He did not see me, of course: spirits have no power to shift matter in this material realm. However, the state of his person left me in no doubt: this was the very same man, with the accretions of six more days upon his tunic.

I looked around again, and what I saw would have made my blood run cold had I not been insanguinal. At the foot of the wall, well sheltered from the wind, was a long black patch. I knew at once what must have happened.

Can you imagine? That fool of a boy had burned my body. He had decided that I was not going to come back. There was nothing left of me but a pile of ashes.

What was I to do? My time in the incarnate world was not completed. I knew from my talk with Lao that I still had work to do. I floated up into the air and looked around for another spirit-home. My luck was bright: only a short distance away, an old beggar lay by the side of the path. I observed him carefully: from the absence of breath, I concluded that he must be dead. Although his clothes were shabby, his shoulders were broad and his face strong-featured. I shrugged metaphorically; things could have been much worse. Swooping down, I insinuated myself into the empty spirit-space.

My new body was comfortable, if a little itchy. The poor fellow was obviously not accustomed to wash. My hair was matted and hung over my eyes: it would have to be trimmed. I shook my head to clear the fug of alcohol. My hands were large and well-sinewed. My arms were long and muscular. I noted a hole in my tunic: I would have trouble convincing anyone that this manifestation was my usually dapper self. I tried to stand, but my leg twisted beneath me. The poor fellow had to beg because he was lame... Poor fellow? Goodness me, I was talking about myself.

Well, Lang was to blame and he would have to help me adapt. Not that I was angry with the lad when I realized what had happened. Apparently on the seventh day he received word that his mother lay dying. Now, young Lang assumed that I must have attained enlightenment and he had not wanted to dishonour my body by leaving it unattended. Consequently he disposed of it carefully with the proper ceremonies. Commendable and seemly behaviour, although on this occasion it had unfortunate consequences for myself. He then rushed back home to his mother like a good son should. I followed him as fast as my lame leg could carry me. The woman had died shortly before I arrived and the whole family were prostrate with grief. I hobbled through and had a good look at her. Her jaw was lolling open, and I tipped a little water from my gourd into her mouth. She coughed and spluttered, and they all sat up and began to cry harder than ever. To cut a long story short, Lang's mother lived long enough to be a blessing to her daughter-in-law.

When Lao heard what had happened, he laughed until he collapsed in hiccups. I really did not think it was very funny. Oh wise one, I said, how am I meant to do my work with this handicap? When he had calmed down, Lao was a bit more sympathetic. He had this crutch made for me to get around, and I must say it serves very well. The gourd is rather fine too, don't you think? I always have it with me to carry my medicines.

Wisdom, you say? I don't feel terribly wise. They say that the more you know, the more you are aware of your own ignorance. I feel overwhelmed by what I don't know. So maybe that makes me wise in the contrary definition of the word.

Immortal, you ask? Well, obviously I'm immortal. I'm talking to you eight hundred years after I was born. If that doesn't make me immortal, I don't know what does.

****

Think about...

What do you think of the old man in this story? Does he deserve the epithet of 'wise'?

What does the term 'wise' mean to you? What does the old man achieve? What price does he pay for this achievement?

How do you feel if your own body lets you down? How important is your physical self-image at different points of your life? Does this reflect wisdom or resignation?

Does the old man remind you of anyone you know? What is your connection with this person? How do you feel about this relationship?

Have you ever played the part of the wise man? How was your advice received? What effect did it have? How did you feel in this role?

Task

Whether you were aware of it at the time or not, many people have helped and advised you along the way. When you are a child, you take the attention of parents and teachers for granted. It is only as you grow older yourself that you become aware of how important this contribution was.

Think of someone who has been a 'wise man' for you: someone who has given you their time or advice, with no great benefit to themselves. This might be a grandparent, a senior colleague, even just a trusted friend. You probably never told them how much their help meant to you. Even if they are no longer a part of your world, it is never too late to be grateful. Write a letter to them expressing your thanks and appre-ciation for all they have done. If you dare, and if it is still possible, send it to them.

When we acknowledge our mentors in this way, we repay the debt in kind. We also increase the value of the original gift. This process operates in the same way as prayer: by counting our blessings, we remind ourselves of how lucky we are.

12. The Ogre

The figure of the ogre evokes our deepest fears. His very name is a synonym for terror. His dark shape prowls our dreams and haunts our waking hours. He knows no kindness, no mercy, no remorse: only his own hideous hungers spur him on. We dread his presence with a horror which seems to summon him. He is the fiend who lurks at the door, who skulks at the edge of sleep, who prowls at the perimeters of our consciousness. He is the monster who inhabits the darkest corners of our minds.

The figure of the ogre is the opposite of wise old man. Because he represents a threat to us, we have learned to recognize him easily. When we thrill to the score of a horror film, it is because we apprehend his imminent arrival. The devil, the vampire and the murderer are manifestations of this evil form. Dictators such as Hitler, Stalin and Pol Pot incarnate him in human shape. He is so dreadful that we cannot even look this creature in the face. It is our own panic which gives the ogre his awful power. When we hate and fear something beyond rational explanation, we talk of 'demonizing' it. By ascribing the forces of the dark archetype, we give the beast a strength it did not have before. If we turn and face the monster we will find that he is not omnipotent after all. We must not deny the power of the dark side but nor should we exaggerate it.

A less threatening manifestation of this dark archetype is the tramp. Where the ogre is night-black, the tramp is merely a dirty shade of grey. A shabby and sometimes malevolent figure, he represents a life at best wasted and at worst abused. Whilst the wizard has derived wisdom from his experiences, the tramp has nothing to show for his travails. Where the wise king has accumulated riches signifying worth and knowledge, the tramp only owns what he can carry in his bundle. We fear that this paucity of possessions symbolizes failure to learn the universal lessons of life. The real-life tramp may be pitied but he is more likely to be feared. His obstinate refusal to participate in society signifies a dangerous tendency to violate the rules. His lack of respect for worldly goods renders the principle of ownership potentially worthless. The tramp poses a real threat to those with whom he comes into contact: either he is a potential thief, or he represents a code of values which renders their achievements meaningless.[1]

Another common presentation of the ogre is the monstrous figure of the troll. These grotesque creatures are humanoid in shape, but by nature they are lumpen clods. Trolls do not share our motives or emotions. By categorizing them as 'other' we ascribe them sub-human status. As such, they are a ready vessel for our worst fears and unconscious prejudices. Assuming that the troll wants to devour us, we categorize him as a congenital enemy. In this way we preclude the possibility of reconciliation or even friendship. Too often we are guilty of doing this to anyone who seems different to ourselves. This is the old problem faced by minority communities everywhere. Whenever we project malign intentions onto another group we absolve ourselves of any mutual bonds of obligation. The following story of the Mountain King draws on these primal fears of the unknown.[2]

In Scandinavia, belief in trolls was commonplace in rural areas well into the last century. According to Norse mythology the bright gods included both warrior and fertility deities. These were in constant conflict with the frost giants, who represented the chaotic forces of nature. The gods and giants therefore represent powerful elements of the natural world. When the advent of Christianity relegated old beliefs to the category of superstition, the memory of these beings lived on in folk-tales about elves and trolls. If we take these as metaphors for forces which we do not fully understand, we can see that it is eminently sensible to respect their existence. Even today Icelanders will accord such beings serious consideration: if disturbed they may provoke unexplained landslides, and roads have been moved to avoid this. It is quite credible that an unwary traveller on a winter's night might glimpse things that he had better not have seen.

The Mountain King

(A Scandinavian Story)

It had been a long day at market and I was late leaving town. Already dusk was falling and snowflakes danced on the winter wind. The road was a dark strip in the night, ridges of frozen mud to turn your ankle. Soon it disappeared altogether with nothing to mark the way but the odd tree or guidestone. The walk is a hard one and that night it seemed worse than ever before. The wind picked up along the valley, tugging at my coat and making my nose run. The snowfall grew thicker till it beat in my face like swan's wings. There was no way then to tell where the path might lie, but I knew better than to stop. Never stand still in a winter storm: the ice giants are out, hurling their great boulders at any man they see. Your only chance is to keep going and hope to find shelter of some kind.

Stumbling up the hill, I almost fell against a tumble of rocks. I felt along until I found a space between two boulders. The snow was thinner here and the stones gave some protection from the storm. I burrowed down into the dry grass, trying to make some sort of den. It fell away beneath my hands and there before me was a crack in the hillside. The wind clawed like a wild thing at my back but the cleft was dark and still. I pulled my coat tight around me and crawled inside.

The walls of rock led back into the hillside, forming a natural tunnel. The going was easy, for the floor was smooth as if it had been levelled. After a while the air seemed to grow warmer and there was a faint glow ahead. Muffled noises drifted down the passageway – harsh voices, scraping and banging sounds. At the end of the corridor was an archway and I stumbled towards it. Pressing myself against the coarse stone, I peered cautiously out.

Hidden there in the heart of the mountain lay a great hall. Its roof was carved from the living rock and sparkled with a thousand crystals. The walls were roughly quarried and covered with moving shadows. The room was lit with flaming torches held in immense iron brackets. Down the centre of the hall ran a long stone table heaped with food. Huge trenchers of meat were interspersed with great piles of jewelled fruit. The diners at this feast were mountain trolls, with great flat faces and hairy hands. They gnawed the flesh with yellow teeth and as they ate, they flung the bones to the floor. At the head of the table sat the troll king, most hideous of them all. He lolled in his chair, grinning horribly at the festivities.

Serving maids moved around the table, filling platters and replenishing empty cups. As she passed, one of these saw me standing in the opening. She picked me up like a doll and stroked my hair. Smirking furtively, she held me close before her eyes.

"What's a pretty one like you doing here?" she giggled. "A tasty morsel you'd make for my liege lord. But no, he shall not have you tonight. I'll be keeping you for myself, my poppet."

She dropped me in the pocket of her apron and turned back to her duties. It was dark in there, and the stench of her was stifling. As she moved around the hall, her skirt swung against her legs till I was bruised and sore. I durst not cry out, for fear of what would happen if I were discovered.

She went one time to fill the troll king's cup, and he spoke in a voice like rocks splitting.

"Come closer, my dear. What have you there in your pocket?"

Her hand came in and caressed me, whilst she tossed her head flirtatiously.

"Why, 'tis my babe, and have you seen his silky hair? Just like mine, is't not?"

"Come here and let me feel, my lovely."

He grabbed at her and she skipped away, gurgling like a geyser.

Soon after that the music started, great booming sounds that shook the sides of the mountain. The table was pushed back against the wall and the dancing began. Trolls stamped and spun, slowly at first, then faster and faster. Soon the whole hall was filled with huge swaying figures. The troll maid grasped me to her breast and joined the dance. I thought to die gripped in those great rough hands, her breath hot against my ear. It was an age before the tune ended and the musicians exchanged their instruments for drink. The troll dancers fell to the floor, gasping and groaning with pleasure. Smiling at nothing, their eyes closed and they began to snore.

When all was quiet, I freed myself from the troll maid's embrace. The torches had burned low, but there was enough light to see the door at one end of the hall. I paused to fill my pockets with the jewelled fruit, and pick up the smallest of the spoons. It would have made a fine soup-ladle for a human hearth. I thought to take one of the wroughten drinking cups, but it was too heavy for my hold. It fell with a clatter from my hands and rolled along the floor. The troll king stirred and opened one thick-rimmed eye.

"Stop thief!" he cried, and at once the other trolls awoke.

I ran down the hall and came to the great door. It was too heavy for me to move, but there was a narrow gap underneath. I dropped the spoon and squeezed through the crack. My coat caught and I lost some buttons, but in a moment I was out and running down the passageway beyond. Behind me I heard grating hinges, then the thud of thick-skinned feet. A rasp of rough voices were raised in a hunting cry. My heart was pounding fit to burst and the breath burned in my throat. Ahead of me was a lighter space, and suddenly I found myself in the open air. I went tumbling down the hillside like a child learning to walk. Behind me the yells grew louder, then suddenly stopped. The morning sun was stretching down the valley, and as it touched the trolls they turned to stone. Where they had been was nothing but a straggle of boulders strewn down the slope.

I gathered myself together and looked around. Surely this

place was familiar, for it was the pasture just above our farmstead. That whole dreadful time I'd been only a cat's walk from home. In the morning light it was hard to believe myself what I had seen. I reached into my pocket, but instead of jewels all I pulled out was a handful of coal. Now, you can believe me or not, since I've never been back to find that cave nor never wanted to: but for sure the mountain king is still feasting down there in his great hall beneath the hills.

******

Think about...

When do you think this story takes place? How does the setting influence the story?

Why do you think this story was first told? What does it purport to explain? What questions does it raise? How well does it deal with these issues?

What does other stories does this one remind you of?

Can you think of any modern parallels to this story? How does the media 'demonize' those whom we fear? Why does society do this? To what extent is propaganda justified?

Have you ever found yourself in a similar situation to this benighted traveller? How did you come to be in this position? Were your prejudices reinforced or challenged by the experience?

What does the figure of the Troll King mean to you? Is he a real person or a feeling inside? Who in your life represents this archetype? How do you feel towards this person? Why do you feel this way?

Task

When you categorize someone as 'other', you preclude the possibility of ever seeing things from their point of view. If you try to understand their perspective, they may not seem so frightening after all.

Many myths tell of a hero who fights a monster. Theseus kills the Minotaur; Perseus slays snake-haired Medusa; Beowulf destroys

Grendel and his monstrous mother. These creatures are half-human, but hideous beyond belief. Often these demons are female, but they are shown no mercy on that account. The role of the hero is to conquer: that of the monster, to be overcome.

When you know a little more about the monster, you may begin to feel differently. The Minotaur has a bull's head because his father withheld a sacrifice from the gods; Medusa was once a pretty girl whose actions displeased a goddess; Grendel's mother sacrifices her life in an attempt to avenge her son. If you know the story of Frankenstein, you pity the lonely hybrid he created. Maybe you can even identify a little with the beast.

Choose a myth with a scary monster. Write about what happens in your own words - from the viewpoint of the beast. Imagine how it feels to be this creature. What have you experienced? How has this affected you? How do you think other people see you? What have you done, or left undone? Why did you behave in this way? Use the first person ("I thought... I felt... I did..."). Labelled a monster, you never had a chance. Tell us your side of the story.

Warning*: This is an extremely powerful exercise. It may evoke deeply submerged thoughts and feelings which are hard to manage. Once the story has been told, you must disengage from the monster. When you have finished writing, lay down you pen and exhale deeply. Breathe out the residue of emotion from your stomach. Stand up slowly and move away from the place where you have been working. Wash your hands in cold running water and shake off the drops. Have a drink and perhaps something to eat. Give yourself time to integrate what you have learned with your 'real' self.*

This experience is also deeply empowering. Through identifying with the monster, you may learn that he is actually an aspect of yourself. When you face your fears, you no longer have to project them onto someone else. In acknowledging your own dark side, you can counteract your distrust of the darkness outside. If you can make peace with your inner demons, you can use their powers to help you.

Archetypal Stories

Good stories are hard to suppress. The more dramatic the tale, the better: scandal and gossip travel faster than good news. Stories tell us what has happened in the past and how it impacts on the present. In storytelling traditions, the same subjects tend to recur across time and between cultures. Tales of heroes fighting dragons or poor girls marrying a prince appeal to something deep within all of us. Details of narrative or characterization may differ, but the dominant themes and major events appear in places separated by many thousands of miles. Stories are a window onto another level of reality: we recognize their validity irrespective of the form in which we first encounter them. This is true for both secular stories and sacred narrative. The same truth may manifest in many national costumes, but they all convey the same underlying message.

There are some stories which occur so often and have so many common features that they seem to be of universal interest. Typically these stories address profound philosophical questions which have concerned people in all places and from earliest times. They have spread so widely and survived so long because they have adapted universal themes to local forms. They deal with existential questions in the guise of specific concerns. Myths present a surface story which also has a latent meaning. A descent to the Underworld symbolizes seeking the wisdom of the unconscious mind. The son is a manifestation of a possible future self. The journey is a metaphor for personal development: the voyage is more important than the destination itself.

These themes manifest in our everyday lives. The nightclub where we use alcohol as an excuse for honesty; the football dad screaming at his five-year-old avatar; the holidays where stories of surviving disaster are more vivid than memories of famous sights. They also appear in good writing. The best books explore profound philosophical issues in the guise of a simple story. Novelists and scriptwriters select specific plots which allow them to address universal questions. The exploration and elaboration of fundamental concerns through stories is one of the basic features of human culture.[1]

Stories of creation, of great floods, of heroic achievement – these take many forms, but we recognize them wherever we encounter them. Appearing across time and culture, they evoke response on a profound level. These themes recur so widely that they must resonate with templates deep in our unconscious minds. It is therefore is proper to call such stories 'archetypal'.

Appendix B: Travelling Tales explains why similar stories appear in different places.

13. Creation and Re-Creation

Creation stories try to explain the origins of this manifest world and of its human inhabitants. Like all myths they have multiple levels of meaning. Many traditions echo the creation myth of Western science, with life emerging from the primordial deep. This image is a very powerful one. Water is the element of the Goddess: the Great Mother gives birth to all things, often starting with the first generation of gods. This image of original creation mirrors the emergence of the individual child from the waters of the womb. We are thus all children of the divine feminine.

Mankind is often said to have been formed out of mud or clay by a creator deity who then breathed life into the figures. It may seem strange to us for people to be made of dirt. When the Ku Klux Klan referred to non-whites as 'mud people', they meant it to sound derogatory. However, for most of history earth has been the main source of human food and so of sustenance. To say that we are made of clay is simply to acknowledge our incarnate physical nature. Sometimes the maker god takes an ongoing interest in his work; in other cases, he loses interest and retreats to a distant abode in the sky. In many African stories, the creator being is a sky god. Disappointed with mankind, he withdrew leaving people to take care of themselves. In some traditions, this world is the only attempt at creation; in others, it is simply one of a succession of worlds, each of which is destroyed at the appointed time.[1]

Stories of great floods occur widely across the world. In many traditions, previous worlds were typically washed away in a terrible deluge. In some cases this may reflect distant folk memories of inundation by great rivers, or of coastal waters rising at the end of the last Ice Age. However, Flood stories also occur among peoples who live in mountainous regions far removed from the sea. The persistence and widespread occurrence of these stories shows that they resonate with something deep in the human psyche. Water represents the eternal feminine principle: constantly changing form and appearance, it appears to yield but always finds its true level. The Flood represents the powers of the Goddess in full flow. In cinematic convention waves are often used to symbolize overwhelming passion. The rising waters of the inundation also symbolize the powers of the unconscious mind. We cannot fight these forces with logic since they represent an inalienable part of ourselves. Sometimes we must be willing to surrender the power of the intellect and follow the instincts which may be the wisest part of ourselves.

The Flood is another kind of Creation story: it represents an opportunity to make the world anew. Post-apocalyptic survival scenarios are the modern versions of this myth. Stories of creation and recreation have an obvious metaphysical angle: they are about constructing identity and new beginnings. Myth reminds us that it is always possible to make a fresh start. Images of death and rebirth portray the eternal renewal of life, often symbolized by the phoenix. Even when we achieve our heart's desire it is not in human nature to rest content for long. We could always move to the country, or change jobs, or have plastic surgery. Change is a sign that we are still players in the great game of life. The mythic imagination is not satisfied with living 'happily ever after'. Like a cosmic kaleidoscope, it constantly throws new elements together to ask, 'What if...?'

Some of the earliest stories in the world come from Mesopotamia, in the area we now call the Middle East. Mesopotamia is a Greek word meaning 'the land between two rivers'. It was on the fertile plain between the Tigris and Euphrates that people first learned how to farm crops. These great rivers were key to the way of life in the region. Every year after the spring rains they flooded, leaving the soil rich with alluvial silt. Soon people were producing more food than they could eat. The surplus was traded for other goods and the region became wealthy and powerful. The land of Sumer lay in the south; to the north was Akkad, with the great cities of Babylon and Nineveh. According to the written traditions of Sumeria and Babylon, the Great Flood constituted the first major landmark in historical time. Before the Flood, legendary kings reigned for thousands of years; afterwards, rulers were ascribed a human-scale span of time.[2]

Atrahasis and the Great Flood

(A Mesopotamian Myth)

In the days when the world was young, there were greater gods and there were lesser gods; and the lesser had to work for the glory of the greater. At the beginning this did not cause any problems; but eventually the lesser gods became tired of their toil, and they grew sullen and resentful.

Enlil, the Supreme Being, saw that the gods were discontent and was troubled in his heart. He summoned a council of the wisest gods and asked them for advice. The gods deliberated long and hard about the problem. At last Enki, the god of water, had an idea. The crafty one proposed that the gods make mankind, so that they might labour on behalf the gods, and praise them, and give them offerings. The mother goddess took clay and mixed it with divine blood. She fashioned the clay into little figurines, some male and some female. From the clay seven couples were made, with the power of procreation.

This was indeed a clever solution. Mankind laboured to produce food from the land; they praised the gods and made offerings. For a while all was well, and the gods were satisfied.

But over time, the numbers of people grew until they filled the earth and the air with their clamour, and the gods could not sleep for the noise. The humans who had been a boon were now an irritation. Enlil became angry at the constant disturbance. He decided to send a plague to decimate mankind.

However, Enki was proud of his creation and did not want them destroyed. There was one man of whom Enki was particularly fond, whose name was Atrahasis. He was a wise man, well respected by his neighbours. Enki instructed Atrahasis to tell the people to make offerings of grain and stay very quiet. The noise suddenly abated; the gods feasted contentedly on their offerings; and Enlil relented and withdrew his decree.

But over time the people forgot and their numbers increased, and again their clamour rose to fill the heavens. This time Enlil sent a famine to destroy them, and many people died; but the noise of the survivors wailing only grew louder.

Enlil was angered that his plan had failed. He determined to finally eradicate the human race. This time he decided to send a great flood to destroy mankind. And this time he made the gods swear that they would not warn the people of his plans.

Atrahasis had been working all morning. He was tired: even a good man can get tired, especially a good man who has been working for hours. While his wife prepared lunch, he went to lie down on his bed. The house was built of reeds and mud, in the style of the country; it was cool and restful after a hard day's work.

Enki had vowed that he would not warn Atrahasis of the forthcoming flood. A god does not break his vow. Instead, the wise one used his cunning. As Atrahasis slept, Enki stood outside and whispered to the reed wall. A deluge is coming, he confided to the wall. It can only be survived by one who dismantles his house and builds a boat with two decks, using tar to seal the gaps between the timbers, and gathers their family and livestock inside.

Atrahasis woke from his sleep in a cold sweat. The dream had been so vivid: surely Enki had been speaking to him. He sprang up and rushed outside. The sky still seemed blue, the sun as bright as ever: but the memory of his vision was strong in his mind. He knew well enough the damage that a flood could do. Each year the river burst its banks, bringing precious silt and moisture to the fields: but a great deluge that covered the houses too would be disastrous. Ignoring the rumblings of his stomach, Atrahasis stalked around the house. Would it be possible to do as the god instructed? There was not much timber in these low-lying lands, but a few small trees grew. Perhaps a raft made of reeds lashed together, as they often used to cross the river? But it would have to be larger than any raft he had seen before. Two rafts, possibly, with curved sides and partitions for the livestock? He would have to start construction at once, and do as best he could.

Atrahasis worked day and night to build his craft. As the clouds gathered, he gathered his family together and led them on board. He also took both wild and domestic animals as instructed by the god.

The sun disappeared and there was total darkness. The wind howled, and rain descended in torrents. The flood waters rose and engulfed the world. Atrahasis and his family were safe but the rest of humanity was reduced to a pile of mud. The boat drifted for seven days and nights with its cargo of people and animals before it finally ran aground.

At last the waters subsided, and Atrahasis came out from his boat. His first act was to build an altar and make devout offerings to the gods in thanks for his salvation. Enlil smelled the smoke from the sacrifice and realized that someone must have survived the flood. Furious that he had been tricked, he raised his voice in angry threats. However, Enki soothed him, pointing out that without mankind, there would be no-one to labour for the gods and make them offerings. Enlil could see the logic of this argument and was placated. With a great show of reluctance, he agreed to let the survivors live. Moreover, he rather admired the spirit and wisdom of this one man.

He granted Atrahasis and his wife the gift of eternal life.

******

Think about...

Why do people tell Creation stories? What are they trying to explain? What other Creation stories do you know? What are the similarities with this story? Why do you think these common features occur? Are there any important differences? What do these stories show us about the people who first told them?

What other versions have you heard of the Flood story? Compare and contrast these stories. When and where was each story set? Why did the floods occur? Who was saved, and why? Why do you think stories like this are so widely told? Do you think they refer to real historical events, or are they elaborate metaphors for something else? What do these stories mean to you?

Task

Stories of creation and re-creation reveal important things about the human psyche. Above all, they remind you of the joy of being alive. You are born into this world for an allotted time, but most of the time you behave as if you were going to live for ever. The purpose of incarnate existence is the ability to feel and to act. Cast adrift upon the waters, the flood survivors exist in a state of suspension like someone in a flotation tank. Only when the water subsides can they resume any meaningful activity. This is similar to the sensation you may sometimes have on holiday: a tropical paradise is wonderful, but after a while you start to crave some sense of purpose in life.

What do you enjoy about being incarnate? We do not live on earth for long, so we better make the most of it. Write down a few of your favourite things. Focus on your five senses: what do you love to see, to hear, to smell, to taste, to touch? List your favourite activities: do you enjoy paragliding, or just a walk in the park? Maria in 'The Sound of Music' got it absolutely right: just thinking about our favourite things can make us feel better.

When did you last do or feel these things? Plan to get some of these good experiences into your life again soon. Be specific: picture the event and set a date to do it. We only have one life that we know about, so we might as well enjoy it! As the saying goes, yesterday is a memory; tomorrow is a dream; but today is a gift – that's why we call it the present.

Choose one of these special experiences. What words would you choose to describe it? Write a poem about your favourite thing.

Part III

Personal Mythology

There are two questions that we have to ask ourselves in life. The first is "Where am I going?" and the second is "Who will go with me?" The important thing is to get these questions in the right order.... [1]

Myth and Archetype

Human beings are natural born storytellers. We perceive pattern and meaning in the co-incidence of events. On the physical level, our bodies are programmed to structure basic elements into complex forms. Strings of genes determine our development from within the womb. In cognitive terms we respond instinctively to shape and sequence. Infants can identify the distinctive sounds of human speech and use them for communication. We see pictures in tea-leaves and dancing figures in flickering flames. Similarly, people have an innate ability to take the basic building blocks of narrative and construct them into a coherent story-line. The oldest manifestations of story are to be found in myths; the latest are the newly-composed narratives of our own lives.

Modern books, plays and films draw on classic mythic themes. Myths show us a model of the world. They tell us of events and actions which make sense in relation to one another. Mythologies consist of both characters and narratives, or archetypes and myths. When we speak of 'Greek mythology', we are referring to a body of stories about a particular set of gods and heroes. Some characters, like Herakles, have many adventures; sometimes different characters have similar stories, like Perseus and Theseus. A particular mythology might not correspond to our own life experiences – modern monsters may not breathe fire

– but it will have internal consistency. When we understand the society in which it developed, we can appreciate it on its own terms. It is because the stories within a given mythology relate to one another that myths are collectively more useful to us than folk or fairy tales.

Myths are collective constructs which help us to find individual meaning in the world. They tell us about things that have happened once before and could happen again. Myths make us feel that our personal experiences and insights are valid and universal. They reassure us that our lives have meaning and purpose. They inspire us to carry on even in difficult times. They help us to see patterns in our own lives, and understand how we have reached the place where we find ourselves. Myths also have a proactive function: the insights gained from stories help us to plan the future, using narrative templates as a charter for future actions.

The process by which we do this is an alchemistic one. Our culture provides works of reference to help us compose our life plans. Old stories preserve the wisdom of those who have gone before. They are travellers' tales, telling us what other people experienced along the way. We can learn of the dangers they faced, how they responded and what the outcomes were for them. But having a map is not the same as undertaking the journey yourself. The signpost is not the destination; it claims to offer no more than guidance. The ancient charts warn that 'here be dragons' and fade away towards the edges of the world. We can study them avidly, but must each eventually set out on our own personal journey.

Our stories typically contain a standard repertoire of stock characters. We base these characters on primal figures which arise spontaneously within the human mind. These figures are of course the psychic forms which Jung called archetypes. They consist of clusters of attributes which we project onto those around us, eliciting behaviour in line with our expectations. The archetypes are modified and elaborated on the basis of personal experience. We give a face to the kind old woman based on our image of a grandmother. The hero bears a remarkable similarity to whichever film star is currently in the ascendant. The archetypal figures provide us with roles for the people in our lives. These figures must then be given a function in our stories: this is the principle of synthesis, by which the players are brought to life and develop relationships with each other. We draw on myth and archetype to develop our personal mythologies.

Exercise A: Encountering Archetypal Figures shows the roles which people around you play in your life.

The Power of Stories

Each of us has as story to tell. That is who we are: we define ourselves in terms of our story. We have chosen the settings and many of the characters. The narrative is selectively edited to suit our circumstances and our self-image. Certain events and actions are recalled with pride; others are regarded as untypical, and best forgotten. Some things happened to us that were not planned: we were victims, but survived through luck and resourcefulness. Both consciously and unconsciously we edit our experiences in line with our expectations. We tell anecdotes which create a structure and sequence from chance events. On the basis of these accounts we construct both a public persona and a private self.

Storytelling is a skilled craft. Narrators use tricks and techniques (the power of repetition, the rule of threes) to hold our attention and build suspense. Most importantly, the story chosen must be relevant to the audience. A tale well told should be both beautiful and functional. When we hear other stories, we gain knowledge of things outside our own immediate experience. The stories we come across give us insights gleaned from the lives of others. They give us understanding of how others think and perceive the world; they inform our expectations of new circumstances; and they help to form our ideals, our aspirations and our dreams. We use material from stories we have heard to interpret our memories, understand our experiences and plan future encounters. As we grow, the narratives we encounter – both our own life experience and tales we have been told or read – help to make us who we are.

The stories that we hear may have a number of different functions. At the manifest or surface level, they offer explanation or instruction about the world. They provide role models who personify different types of attitude and behaviour. They demonstrate the possible consequences of choices and actions and offer either a good example or a terrible warning. At the latent level they can be interpreted symbolically, containing metaphors and allegories which speak to the human soul. When we hear a story we usually recognize and respond to the literal content (events and overt motives) but may not be aware at a conscious level of the deeper psychological implications of the tale.

We draw on universal themes to construct our individual stories. A story can be defined as a narrative sequence of events. The various incidents are linked together so as to imply meaningful connection. The causal structure of narrative imparts a sense of significance to our lives. Our life plans are crafted in the same way as great literature. Novelists and scriptwriters use similar techniques to the myth-makers of old. All stories employ narrative as a presentational device. Events occur in a causal sequence: in other words, one thing is shown as leading to another. This reflects human experience of the phenomenal world. We use our memories to construct a linear series of events which is more important in our minds than the annual cycle of the seasons. Stories are the primary intimation of order in human existence.

The most significant forms in which we encounter stories are myth and its little sibling, folk-tale. These traditional tales preserve the oldest stories known to man, and provide the prototype from which all other forms of narrative derive. They address universal concerns – friendship and bravery; life and death – which are still important to us today. Myths endure because they have a perceived personal significance for everyone. They are empowering because they operate at the level of the individual. They give us a blueprint for how to think, feel and behave. The actions and events portrayed provide metaphorical models of desirable behaviour. Myths are descriptive, not prescriptive: they show us the possible consequences of our actions, but they do not tell us what to do. They deal with existential issues and feature archetypal characters which resonate with our own experience. Because of this, they provide an especially rich source of information with which we can work. Myths furnish us with both the characters and the narrative templates to construct our own stories. In this sense, we are all made in the image of the gods.[2]

Stories involve both narrative and character. The plot depends in part upon the people who appear in it; the personalities of those people derive in part from the story in which they find themselves. The tales we hear as children provide us with role models from which we construct a persona for ourselves. *Persona* is the Latin word for a mask, worn onstage to indicate the actor's role. If 'all the world's a stage' then our lives consists of acting out the parts we have identified for ourselves. We select our personas and venture forth to engage into the world. The parts which we can play are determined largely by our archetypal heritage. Our actual choice is in turn influenced by social factors including cultural constraints and economic conditions. The dramas which we choose to enact depend mainly upon our dominant life script.[3]

We tell stories to make sense of our lives. Our personal stories are influenced by the narratives we have encountered. Tales which resonate with us provide a template of reality which informs our choices and affects our actions. We are shaped and influenced by the stories we hear, especially when young: Beauty and the Beast; Cinderella; Florence Nightingale – these still have the power to determine our decisions in adult life. The same process operates at the level of the nation-state. Our Greco-Roman socio-political heritage provides an ideology which is utilized by politicians to induce an emotional response ('The hero will protect the poor / avenge his father's murder'). We have also introduced a few modern variants of our own ('Technology can provide you with personal salvation'; 'Only the young are worthy'). If history can provide the original material for myths, then myths can also make history. On both a personal and a national level myths provide the models by which we make sense of the world.

Exercise B: Identifying Life Themes helps you to see the dominant influences in your personal story.

Table 2: Traditional Stories

	FolkTale	Legend	Myth
When set	Any time / timeless	Long ago/olden days	Before history began
Characters	Mortal + magical beings	Heroes + monsters	Gods, heroes + mortals
Where set	Any place, often rural	World as we know it	Earlier /sacred world
Where told	Social situation	Educational context	Structured / ritual setting
Why told	Practical purpose: Entertainment	Instructional aim: Inspiration	Spiritual / Psychological: Insight
Status	Secular ←——————————→ Sacred		

Using Words and Pictures

We construct an inner vision of reality which enables us to function in the external world. The information we gain from our senses is supplemented by material from the unconscious mind. If we want to operate effectively we must recognize these two types of knowledge. Our image of the world must reflect outward conditions, whilst acknowledging the forces that make us unique. One of the main goals of psychotherapy is to 'make the unconscious conscious'. This aim is in line with the basic tenets of spiritual development as practised in all the major world religions. The writer M. Scott Peck has defined spiritual growth as the growth or evolution of consciousness. To achieve this, the rational conscious mind must learn to work in harmony with the wisdom of the unconscious.

We all perceive things in different ways: we literally see the world differently from our neighbours. This is because people have different ways of processing facts about the world around them. The way in which you get information from your environment is called your learning style. We have five senses, but the dominant ones are sight and sound: we tend to focus on incoming data in the form of images and words. If you tend to believe the evidence of your eyes then you have a visual learning style. If you prefer to analyze what you have heard or read, you have a verbal learning style. Your dominant learning style affects many aspects of your life. If you have a visual learning style you prefer to learn by watching documentaries on television; you like to spend your free time doing sport or playing music. If you have a verbal learning style, you get information by reading books and newspapers; you probably enjoy writing letters and conversation with friends. Most importantly, your learning style affects the way in which you construct your personal mythology.[4]

Just as we each have a preferred learning style, we tend to structure our personal myths along predominantly either visual or verbal lines. For visual learners, it is the archetypal figures which shine most clearly in their minds. The characters in their lives engage in an eternal dance; the details of daily interaction are of less importance. Relationships for the visual processor are a product of archetypal function. The significant people in their lives may not be aware of the roles they have taken on, any more than the mythmaker is aware of his projections. Each will play their allotted part for better or worse, depending on both their natural personality and external circumstances. For some people, the actual individuals with whom they have relationships are virtually interchangeable. They can uproot their life and move across continents in pursuit of a career, replacing their friends and lovers upon arrival with almost perfect substitutes. Tor the visual-spatial processor this is not hard-heartedness but purely a matter of pragmatism.[5]

For verbal processors the story is paramount. Events in their lives are consciously linked to create a coherent narrative. Their relationships are central to their scripts: the importance of friends and partners depends on their role in the story. It is sometimes said that we draw others into our lives in order to learn from them. It might just as truly be said that we attract others who are willing to learn with us. Verbal processors seek out companions who will join them in the great adventure of life. Relationships for them are a function of shared emotion and common narrative. They make an effort to keep in touch with friends from former times: these are the guardians of a part of their personal history. Although this 'loyalty' is based on selfish motives, it has social and emotional benefits to both parties. The downside of such conservatism is a tendency to over-analyze events, and consequently to worry.

Appendix C: Learning Styles describes these cognitive processes in more detail.

Everyone uses both kinds of learning to some degree. The difference lies in our habitual patterns of analysis and behaviour. We can all gain from trying to see the world differently. If you are a free-spirited spatial processor, you might benefit from paying more attention to detail. If you are an analytic verbal type, you could enjoy liberating your artistic side. We do not use all of the neurons in our brain: our minds have an astonishing plasticity to adapt for optimum performance. If you have a strong tendency towards one type of information processing you can see this, not as a limitation, but as an opportunity for personal growth.

Exercise C: Working With Images draws on your powers of visualization.

Constructing a Personal Mythology

Your life is a story. You are the author of your script, and its main protagonist. You have been working on your script since you were very young. Using fragments of fairy tale and anecdote, you told stories to make sense of the world. As you grew older, your life script became more complicated. You encountered stories in books and films: you used these to develop your personal narrative template. Your script is based on your experiences, but it also determines how you see the world. The choices that you make depend largely upon your life script. The story of your life determines who you are.

Your autobiography is the greatest story you will ever tell. Sometimes it will seem a great adventure; at others, it may feel like a comedy or a bitter satire. Autobiographies show us that 'personal narrative' is a key influence on behaviour. Knowing how a person perceives their own past is one of the best ways of predicting how they will behave in the future. For this reason, it is important for each of us to make sure that the story we construct is empowering, rather than disabling. We have the power to select and interpret elements which enable us to function more effectively in the world. This process of consciously reconstructing our lives incorporating those things which are important to us has been described as 'recovering a sense of identity' (Cameron 1994). This includes both the selection of narrative elements and the identification of characters to whom we allocate ongoing parts in our personal life story.

Life consists of a series of events over which we have varying degrees of control. We navigate to the best of our ability, steering as close as possible to the course of our dreams. To do this we each construct a model of the world which has both explanatory and predictive powers. Your inner model of reality constitutes your 'personal mythology'. It contains a selection of episodes which you re-structure to create an original story, and character descriptions, including detailed delineation of appearance and intention. This dramatic template has internal logic and consistency, although it may not correspond to other people's ideas of external reality. It reconciles your personal experience and cultural heritage with your hopes and plans for the future. This synthesis provides you with a rationale for existence and a blueprint for living.

Your personal mythology allows you to function effectively in the world. It contains stories which direct your actions and characters which you project onto those around you. Your plot is based on fragments of narrative sequence drawn from books, plays and films. You may modify these elements on the basis of actual experience but they form the framework of your story. The parts in your personal drama are played by the people around you who correspond most accurately to the archetypal figures in your mind. You draw on universal themes and common characters to compose your individual script. Your personal mythology is the inner template by which you live your life. It colours your perceptions and guides your actions. It enables you to live your life with integrity.

Your individual story is unique but many of the characters in it are familiar. Figures from the ancient myths still manifest in the modern world. Guardian gods and metaphorical monsters battle each other in our minds. They represent what is best and worst in us, our greatest potential and our deepest fears. In mythical terms, monsters represent not an external threat but a call to action. Without a quest the hero would never leave his hearth. We use conventional characters both to guide our own behaviour and to categorize others. Our images, good and bad, are projected onto those around us. We identify these figures in other people from physical features or behavioural traits: on this basis we ascribe motives and emotions to them. The way we treat others elicits self-confirming responses which justify our initial behaviour. In this way our prejudices and preconceptions are vindicated and reinforced. Of course, the most fearsome enemy is the one already within the walls. We can conceive these terrible images because they reflect something lurking in our subconscious. Every person in your life embodies an aspect of your own psyche. We perceive in others what we carry in our own hearts.

Rather than fearing the darker figures, we can learn to greet them as aspects of our selves. The people who disturb us most provide mirrors in which we may see ourselves. Every archetype is potentially present within each of us. When we act in a particular role, we interact with the archetypal figures innate in those around us and provoke appropriate behaviour from them in response. Your Urchin (Poor Child) may elicit the Good Mother in a friend or partner; your Hero may be spurred to action by an encounter with a Wise Man. By disentangling these relationships and identifying the archetypal patterns underlying them, we are better able to control our projections and manage our own behaviour. We can learn to draw on archetypal images and energies as a power for change.

The process by which you devise a life script and animate the archetypes is a function of your unconscious mind. When you understand how you formed this inner chart, you can assess its objective accuracy and hence it effectiveness as a life tool. A personal mythology is a living creation, not a static model. You can edit those features which are not helpful in your current circumstances. You are free to add or delete elements in your cast and script. When you recognize the influence of archetypes, you can modify the parts ascribed to the people in your personal history. Identifying with strong positive characters can inspire and empower us. Conversely, if someone has a negative impact on your life, you can choose to replace them. Sometimes it is appropriate to walk away from an abusive relationship, but often it is enough simply to alter your archetypal image: prejudice can blind us to positive qualities in another person. Challenging deep-seated beliefs is vital if you intend to change your life script. Your view of the world determines how you behave; your actions in turn influence your experience. Your life choices so far have been based on a combination of personal characteristics and external events. You are a product of your circumstances, but you can determine what happens next.[6]

Exercise D: Developing Your Script helps you identify the stories and characters you want in your personal mythology.

The pattern of your own life is hard to see. You are often too close to view things objectively. A tapestry is woven from the reverse side: the image is only visible once it is turned over. The threads of your life may look similarly tangled until the pattern is complete. It is not always clear where you are going, nor why things turned out the way they did. Life has to be lived forwards but read backwards. The plot of your story – how one thing led to another – is only evident in retrospect. It is difficult to identify the turning points in your own history: apparent adversity can provide a fulcrum for change. Sometimes life seems harsh or unfair, but hard times can provide the greatest lessons.

Although the purpose of life is often obscure, the existential mists do lift occasionally. You will sometimes get a sense that you are 'on track': a conviction that you are doing what you were meant to do. This is often accompanied by a feeling of being your 'real' self, the person whom you were meant to be. When you are living in a way that is true to yourself, you are on course to attaining your true potential. In this state you feel not so much happy as profoundly fulfilled. Your life is suddenly imbued with meaning; you can aim higher and achieve more. This experience can give you a sense of direction even after the moment has passed. It clarifies what is important to you and what you must do to be true to your life purpose. It helps to identify both your self image and your life script.[7]

You only have one life: you might as well make the most of it. In creating a personal mythology, you select a story to live by and choose the characters who will perform it with you. Once you become aware of this process, you can start to take conscious control of your life. You are the main protagonist in your own story. Your personal mythology is the psychic prototype according to which you design and enact your life. You can re-structure your story, re-cast characters or re-interpret events. You are both player and playwright: you can revise your script and offer new parts to different actors. Developing your personal mythology is the work of a lifetime. Some people start this process earlier than others, but they will not finish any sooner. Identifying your life's theme gives a sense of harmony and purpose to existence. It is never too late to be what you might have been.

You are the author of your own drama, and play the principal part: now you can start to direct your own life script.

Exercise E: Constructing a Life Collage shows you how to create a visual image of your life script.

Reference Notes

Part I: Myth and Meaning

1. Carl Gustav Jung (1875-1961) was the son of a Swiss Baptist preacher; his strict spiritual upbringing influenced his later insights. He studied medicine at Zurich, where he also read extensively in philosophy and theology. Jung was an early follower of the pioneering psychoanalyst Sigmund Freud (1856-1939) but disagreed with his emphasis on the importance of childhood sexual experience. Freud argued that all human behaviour is directed by the unconscious mind, which he viewed simply as a repository of repressed and 'forgotten' items. Jung agreed that there is a layer of the unconscious mind which is based on personal experience, and so is unique to each individual. However, Jung argued that this 'personal subconscious' rests on a deeper level which does not derive from individual experience but is inborn. This underlying mental stratum he termed the 'collective unconscious'. It is a shared substrate of psychic data based on the collective memories of the human race. The collective unconscious includes the universal primal forms which Jung called archetypes.

2. *Arch* is a prefix implying chief or leading, for example archbishop. An arche-type is literally a model, either of a material artefact or of a psychological concept, from which copies are made for ordinary use. The concept of original prototypes existing outside the created world is an ancient one. Plato refers to ideal forms which preceded the manifest world, of which the things in this life are but a shadowy reflection. By postulating the presence of such forms within the human psyche, Jung argued that they were all potentially available to everyone. Archetypes in the Jungian sense are primal forms which reside in the uncon-

scious mind. They exist pre-natally and cross-culturally, emerging most clearly in dreams and visions. Their prevalence is shown by their universal manifestation in stories, where they are no longer unconscious but have been transformed into recognizable characters portrayed according to tradition. Archetypes constitute the inherited structure of the psyche: they are the psychological equivalent of instincts. They continually influence our thoughts, feelings and actions. We respond to those around us in line with archetypal expectations, just as certain sequences of behaviour are instinctive in animals. However, archetypes are less prescriptive than animal instincts in that they are only determined as to their form. Jung emphasized that these figures are fluid outlines which we each evolve and elaborate. The content of the primordial image is only determined when it has been filled with the individual material of personal experience.

3. The great world religions use a language of myth and symbolism. A symbol is a sign that has emotional associations in addition to its literal meaning. The Christian cross recalls the crucifix on which Jesus died; it also has connotations of self-sacrifice and represents the intersection of linear time with eternity. An archetype is a figure with the emotional power of a symbol. Religious creators such as Buddha, Christ and Mohammed knew the power of myth and used it to communicate with their followers. However, later adherents were too rigid in their interpretation of the message: this caused what the philosopher Max Weber called 'routinization of charisma' leading to the demise of true religion. Jung felt that traditional Christianity was exhausted, but he became convinced that psychotherapy could take over the role of religion as a route to personal salvation. He believed that what his patients needed was a personal transformation comparable to spiritual enlightenment. For Jung, 'healer' and 'patient' were in a sacred relationship of mutual quest and the spiritual journey was a

lifelong process. Part of his appeal lies in the recognition that the therapist is undergoing a personal journey too. It has been said that if someone was drowning, Freud would throw them a rope; Jung would jump in to swim with them.

4. Early human settlements were typically matriarchal, with the line of descent reckoned through women. Residence was matrilocal, with men moving to live in their wife's family. Food production was the province of women, and hence had to be compatible with childcare: the staple crops were garden produce such as fruit, olives and nuts that could be tended by hand. Farms were managed by women and passed on to their daughters. Often the estate was passed on to the youngest daughter: older girls established their own holdings nearby whilst the last-born (ultimogenitor) remained at home to help her mother. The status of women in these societies was high since they controlled the productive resources of the community. It is easy to understand the attractions of Helen of Troy when we remember that the throne of Sparta came with her hand. The role of men was to provide protection and hunt for animal protein to supplement the basic diet. They were also involved in long-distance travel and trade, leading to the formation of political alliances.

5. Grandam: grand dame – a term of respect for an older woman.

6. The displacement of the Goddess has been argued most coherently by Robert Graves in his seminal book *The White Goddess* (1948). A military man in background and demeanour, Graves was at first sight an unlikely champion of the divine feminine. Nevertheless he was a philogynist, a socialist and a gifted poet. After writing his war memoirs he retired to Deya in Majorca, calling it 'the cheapest corner of Europe'. Here he devoted his work to the Muse who was for him personified by the women in

his life. For Graves, myth is 'a dramatic shorthand record' of actual incidents. The gods and goddesses are based on real people; the events related genuinely occurred, though they may have been exaggerated for narrative effect. What happens in the stories is therefore a coded record of sacred practice and political narrative. The recall, depiction and transcription of events represent a series of transformations by which the early traditions of a culture are preserved. Greek mythology in particular represents a synthesis of religious ritual and historical events.

In ancient times, according to Graves, benevolent matriarchs reigned as moon-queens. They represented the Goddess on earth, and exchanged their ritual consorts at the solstices to maintain the fertility of the godhead. This golden age was shattered by the arrival of patriarchal pastoralist tribes from the north. In accordance with local custom, the sacred king's power was validated by marriage to the moon priestess. Unions between tribal chiefs and sacred queens were accordingly consummated, often by force as recorded in tales of girls abducted by the gods. However, the new sacred kings understandably objected to the accompanying tradition of seasonal ritual sacrifice. The primacy of the moon priestess was therefore appropriated by her male consort and his companions. Since the White Goddess herself had a triple aspect, her divine partner frequently developed complementary personas. These were often portrayed as a triumvirate of brothers, such as Zeus, Poseidon and Hades. Once the roles of the Goddess had been divided and departmentalized, her powers declined commensurately. The triple image of the goddess was replaced by a dual depiction of womanhood, with the beautiful youthful girl portrayed in opposition to the undesirable old hag. The Great Mother was displaced and forgotten, although many of her aspects survive in myth and ritual. Worship of the Goddess endured in practice even though her place in the divine hierarchy was demoted (Homer, for example, portrays Hera as a jealous shrew). The adoration of the Divine Feminine continues into modern times as a parallel strand of religious worship, as shown in the Catholic cult of Our Lady and the many shrines to female saints.

The description of the displacement of the Indo-European Goddess by patriarchal tribes can also be read as an analogy for individual personal development. In psychological terms, each child must evolve from a state of infantile dependency to a position of mature self-reliance. In objective terms, the child has to move from the domestic sphere ruled by women out into the wider (male-dominated) social world. Seen in this way, there is no conflict between the rule of the Moon Goddess and her subsequent eclipse by her son-lover: it is merely a description of the natural succession of the generations.

7. When we dream of a hero we are probably thinking of the 'monomyth' described by Joseph Campbell (1904-1990). Working on his notes for a course in comparative literature, Campbell noticed that the same stories recur in many cultures. Concluding that the features of myth are archetypal and not cultural, he began to study the common psychology of myths from around the world, in particular the image of the hero. Heroism can manifest in many ways. Classic themes are constantly re-enacted in everyday life: 'The latest incarnation of Oedipus, the continued romance of Beauty and the Beast, stand this afternoon on the corner of Forty-second Street and Fifth Avenue, waiting for the traffic lights to change' (Campbell 1949). For Freudian analysts, success consists of attaining independence of one's parents by finding a job and a mate. Jung believed that true maturity only came with the attainment of spiritual insight. For those fixated on the hero ideology, the transition to later life may be problematic. When their physical prowess starts to decline, men often feel redundant. In fact, the heroic role is only the middle stage in a man's life. The good king must combine the features of the hero and the wise man. The powers of the

magician are a compensation which reconciles the former champion with his new role. Only if he learns to accept his limitations gracefully can the hero of any age access true wisdom.

8. Heroes may be the archetypal virile male, but the figure consistently originates in the great pre-literate matriarchal Bronze Age cultures. Archaeological remains ranging from Mohenjo Daro and Harappa in India, Catal Huyuk in Anatolia, Minoan Crete, Malta, and across Europe as far as Ireland indicate a tradition of goddess-worship. The cultic and cultural origins of the hero in matriarchal systems support psychological theories which stress the crucial role of the mother figure in the early formation of the masculine character. In the words of Doctor Spock, a child who is fussed over gets a feeling of destiny; he thinks he is in the world for something important and it gives him drive and confidence. Far from being a patriarchal warrior, the hero is in fact a champion of women. The great Herakles is aptly named 'Glory of Hera', for despite her reported persecution all of his deeds resound to her name. The male of the species is shaped by the hero mythos, which in turn acts as a powerful directive for society in general. The young boy learns that it is his duty to defend his mother, and with her the home whose spirit she encapsulates. This realization is the basis for the transposition of the hero-figure onto everyday life.

9. Berne (1974) first elaborated the concept of 'life scripts'. He postulates that people develop life plans in early childhood based on parental expectations and other influences. Throughout their lives they will continue to seek out friends and partners with interlocking scripts who will play in role, and they will behave in such a way as to elicit script-confirming behaviour from others. Well-rehearsed actions inevitably lead to reiterated consequences, as when a woman becomes involved in a series of violent relationships. This pattern of behaviour is psychologi-

cally destructive, leading to self-confirming hypotheses about the world; it may also even lead to physical harm. In such cases the script needs to be identified and altered to prevent a destructive spiral of behaviour. Berne argues that this can be done through counselling, which can erase the script as a source of predictive behaviour. Script identification (known as Transactional Analysis) is a productive approach to behavioural modification, but it is oversimplified on two counts. Firstly, it recognizes the importance of storyline but ignores the complementary truism that when one script is eradicated it will necessarily be replaced by another. Secondly, it fails to acknowledge the power of archetypal projection in determining human responses.

10. There is an old story which encapsulates this universal truth. A traveller asks an old man about the town he is approaching. His reply is tangential: "What was your last stop like?" The traveller responds enthusiastically, "It was a great town. Good times, friendly people. I was sorry to leave." The old man replies, "You'll find this place much the same". The next passer-by asks the same question but describes his previous stop in bitterly negative terms. He receives the same laconic reply.

Part II: Encountering Archetypes

1. One way to work with stories is to view all the characters as aspects of a single entity. Rather than simply sympathizing with the main protagonist, we can identify with each of the characters in turn. The monster is no longer an external threat, but rather represents our own anger which on occasion threatens to overpower us. The lost child is the inner part of us which seeks reassurance and affection. By trying to understand contrasting and often conflicting characters, we are able to acknowledge their features and sympathize with their needs. All of the figures

in any story can tell us something about our selves. Psychologists say that we suppress those aspects of ourselves which are not socially acceptable or compatible with our self image. Although we may try to deny their existence, these repressed elements of our personality persist and may break through in unpredictable ways, as when we lose our temper or say something inappropriate in a 'Freudian slip'. The psychoanalytic technique of Voice Dialogue tries to reconcile these different parts of ourselves. It is based on Jung's concept of the Shadow, the aspects of our psyche which are rejected as inappropriate by the conscious mind. The Shadow is often projected onto others: when we disapprove excessively of someone, it is often because they express a repressed part of our own personality.

Female Archetypes: The Triple Muse

1. In many traditional cultures, males are associated with action whilst women are portrayed as passive and receptive. The Chinese Taoist image of yin and yang represents these principles in a state of dynamic balance: a perfect circle dissected by a sine curve, producing two interlocking comma-shaped halves. Yin, the dark segment, represents the female element and is associated with water and instinct; yang, the light segment, represents the male element associated with heat and intellect. In each half the opposite element is represented by a small disc, like the eye of a tadpole. This reflects the inter-relatedness of darkness and light. The sun casts shadows; night is illuminated by the light of the moon. From the constant interactive flux of these two complementary principles comes all of creation. Within each individual, whether male or female, activity is made possible by the preceding period of nurture. This succour can be physical, psychological and spiritual. The Goddess may be proactive in her own right, but as the Muse she also provides inspiration for action.

The Princess

1. Modern fables sometimes try to present the princess in a more proactive role. These stories are interesting and often very amusing, but they are in a sense unnecessary. In Jungian terms the princess is an aspect of the anima, the feminine part of the psyche. She is the gentle counterpart of the prince or young hero, who represents the animus or active masculine element. Both of these elements are present in both men and women, although their relative strength varies between individuals. There are times when it is necessary to take positive action, to be an 'actor' in the world; but on other occasions it is more appropriate to wait and see what happens next. As St Francis might have said, we must pray for the wisdom to know the difference.

2. Like the Moon, the young girl is able to leave and return without penalty. It is precisely this characteristic which makes it hard for many young women to settle down. Girls often fantasize of being found by a prince, whom they will marry and live with happily ever after. In reality it is the ability to commit to a relationship, rather than waiting for the perfect partner, which makes fulfilment possible. The act of choice, and the consequent willingness to forgo alternative life paths, is an indication of spiritual maturity. This is most clearly illustrated in the story of 'Beauty and the Beast', where Belle's affection redeems her captor and turns him into the handsome lover of every girl's dreams.

3. The *Ramayana* is popular throughout India and South-East Asia. In Indonesia, shadow-puppet theatres portray the epic adventures. Rama's travels provide an allegory for the journey which each human soul must make. Everyone at some time must endure loss; fight their own demons; and hope to find final redemption. Rama is the ideal king, his life devoted to the

pursuit of duty and the defence of honour. Sita is his faithful consort, embodying the ideal of loving support; she chooses to follow Rama into exile because a wife should stay by her husband's side. Throughout her imprisonment Sita resists Ravana's approaches and remains faithful to her husband. Rama and Sita are finally revealed to be *avatars* or mortal incarnations of the god Vishnu and his divine consort Lakshmi. The marriage of Rama and Sita represents the perfect partnership, committed and loyal. Every Hindu bride is explicitly identified with Sita and her groom with Rama: each couple thus embodies the divine principle of unity.

The Clever Girl

1. These stories probably constitute a folk memory of the indigenous inhabitants of the British Isles, who were driven from more fertile lands by later arrivals. These people had only rudimentary metalworking techniques, which accounts for their fear of iron weapons. They were said to live below the ground, often beneath long low hills called barrows: these are in fact ancient burial mounds. The entrance to a barrow was thought to stand open at certain times of year, when the veil between the co-existing mortal and spirit worlds was thin. These times tended to coincide with important dates in the agricultural cycle. The most significant of these occurred in the spring and after harvest-time. Beltane was a Celtic spring fertility festival when animals were driven through smoke to purify them as they were brought out to pasture. Samhain was a festival at year-end, marked by feasting to celebrate the harvest and consume perishable produce before the long winter. With the coming of Christianity, the old ways were not forgotten but merely transmuted to a more acceptable form. May Day is still a popular time for weddings, festivals and fairs; and we enact protective rituals to dismiss marauding monsters on Hallow's Eve, the night before All Saints' Day.

The Good Mother

1. Sometimes we have to 'mother' a friend or partner when we provide emotional support in times of need. In a healthy relationship this is only a temporary role but during that period the mother archetype is a source of strength enabling us to provide help and reassurance.

2. The old woman who heard the girl cry out completes the triad of female characters in this story. She is Hecate, who represents the third stage of womanhood and the waning aspect of the moon. It is she who knows Persephone's fate, and her knowledge represents the wisdom of the Crone. Her name means 'hundredfold' and recalls that from the darkness of the earth comes the bounteous harvest.

The Wild Woman

1. We crave our mother's love, but we also naturally strive to grow away from her. When we are very young, anything which might take her attention away from us must be challenged. Hobbies, magazines, even our own father may become the subject of our wrath. As we grow older, we still want her dedicated service but would prefer it if her attention was directed elsewhere.

The contrasting images of good and bad motherhood reflect the changing perceptions of the individual child. To the suckling infant the mother is the source of all succour and comfort, but to the rebellious adolescent she represents a constraint from which they must break free. This dichotomy is often represented in fairy stories by the separation of roles between different characters. Thus, Cinderella's real mother was kind and loving; but as her daughter grows, this figure is replaced by a wicked stepmother whose sole intent is to thwart the girl's development.

In this way the child who identifies with the heroine does not have to project dangerous feelings onto their own mother, upon whom in reality they still largely depend.

2. The Great Mother is the central figure in the lunar trinity of maiden, mother and crone. The moon as a source of eternal renewal also carries within her remit the constant knowledge of death. In this aspect, the lunar deity is indeed threatening. The Greek word for moon, *men*, is also the root of the word *menaio*, to rage. The Moon Goddess is respected for her powers, but she also inspires awe to the point of fear. In Hindu art the goddess Kali is shown dancing upon the body of her husband Shiva, wearing a necklace of skulls. Shiva is the god of destruction but his emblem is the lingam, a stone column of phallic significance. Like time itself, Shiva / Kali destroy in order to create: their destructive power implies the reproductive principle. This is dramatically represented in the yin-yang symbol, where the black sector contains an eye of white and vice versa. Creation and destruction, darkness and light alternate in eternal dynamic interplay.

The Grandmother

1. Grandmother's knowledge is typically concerned with our relationship to the natural environment. Her figure manifests in activities which emphasize our bond with nature such as gardening and environmental conservation. As her physical energy diminishes, she uses her wisdom to live in harmony with the world. She has learnt from life that it is easier to swim with a river than against the current; she knows that to catch a wild horse, you have to run alongside it first. Her figure is connected with being rather than doing, with states of existence as opposed to arbitrary actions. Grandmother is a source of deep succour which encourages and empowers those in her care.

2. Many stories start when the father brings home a new wife. To the children of his first marriage this woman will be an imposter until she has earned their trust. Potentially she has all the attributes of the 'bad mother', or wicked stepmother. Fairy stories frequently use this image to explore the changing relationship between mothers and their own adolescent children. During the transitional period, the grandmother's house may provide a place of refuge from the turbulent family home. In his genealogy of the gods, the Greek writer Hesiod tells us that Persephone and Hecate prefer one another's company above all else (*Theogony* 411-52). Granddaughters and grandmothers frequently have a special bond and take great pleasure in their relationship. The communion between the very young and the very old is one of the greatest consolations of age. As the slogan goes, "If I had known grandchildren were this much fun, I would have had them first!"

The Wicked Witch

1. In past centuries, the Christian Church defended itself with a thorough rebuttal of pagan ways. Soon after Christianity became the official religion of Rome in 320AD, other faiths were formally forbidden (although many older traditions survived by adoption, in particular the custom of celebrating Jesus' birthday at the midwinter solstice). In medieval times old women were singled out as a particular threat to the hierarchical religious establishment. In the past, fewer women survived the travails of childbirth: the older female was therefore something of an anomaly, and as such must be suspected of abomination. The witch's large nose is reminiscent of the Jews, clearly enemies of all good Christians. Her knowledge of herbal medicines makes her an obvious source of help in case of medical emergencies: she thus enters into direct competition with the village priest who might alternatively be called upon to administer last rites. For a

peasant family with limited financial resources, the consequences of their choice had to be made starkly clear. The witch's healing powers were seen as unnatural: consequently they must have come from a pact with the devil. In 15th - 17th century Europe, thousands of old women were persecuted as witches. Fortunately the world is a very different place today. The rise in ecological awareness has made people value 'feminine' approaches to knowledge. Environmental policies promote the conservation, rather than exploitation, of nature. The Wicca movement in particular is linked to a resurgence of interest in the old religion of the Goddess (the*a*-logy). With universal education, knowledge is respected rather than feared. The silver generation has reclaimed the ancient image of the wise woman for itself.

2. *Babushki* are concentrically nesting wooden dolls, with a series of successively smaller figures housed inside each other. The largest doll is the Babushka, a Russian term meaning 'little grandmother'.

Male Archetypes: The Great Journey

1. Allowing boys to engage in 'masculine' activities may actually do them good. The archetypes will manifest in us anyway, and gender-stereotypical tasks may prevent them emerging in other behaviour. Cross-cultural studies show that the division of labour in traditional societies – where men engage in agriculture, whilst women cook and take care of children – defuses the extremes of sexually-defined behaviour. Men in sexually egalitarian western countries are more likely to be assertive and competitive, whilst women score more highly on traits of nurturing and neuroticism. It seems likely that the gender-specific activities of 'primitive' hunter-gathering societies evolved to optimize individual behaviour in terms of both productive and social functions. Without the challenges entailed

in everyday survival, men will actively seek out environments in which they can assert their natural assertive and risk-taking tendencies. Placed in a gender-neutral environment, young men join peer groups in which they can demonstrate their physical superiority through sport or more overt conflict situations. Conversely, women feel under increased social pressure to behave in a conscientious and agreeable manner (Schmitt et al 2008).

The very traits which promote survival in less technologically sophisticated societies may be actually detrimental in more settled communities. One of the most common childhood problems in western society is ADHD (Attention Deficit Hyperactive Disorder), which is linked to the DRD4 gene. The prevalence of ADHD suggests that the gene must at some point have conferred survival value. A study of Kenyan Ariaal tribesmen found that men with the gene who live as nomads have well-nourished families, since they regularly scan their surroundings in search of food. However, those who move to towns have difficulty settling into work or formal education: they are consequently more likely to suffer from malnutrition (Eisenberg et al 2008). The characteristics which are an advantage in one set of circumstances can cause problems in a different environment. The trick is not only to know yourself, but to select your path in life accordingly.

The Infant Prince

1. Cedric Errol learns that his grandfather is Lord Fauntleroy. Tarzan is the long-lost Viscount Greystoke.

The Urchin

1. *The Worn-Out Shoes* is similar to the story of *The Twelve Dancing Princesses*, related by the Brothers Grimm. Twelve is a magical

number in many traditions, for it is the product of three times four. Four is the number of cardinal directions (the points of the compass), and so represents the earthly plane. There are four seasons, four elements and four phases of the moon. Three represents the triple realms of heaven, earth and the underworld: it thus conveys intellectual order and spiritual unity. Time is threefold, being divided into past, present and future. The divine is often perceived as having three aspects united in one godhead: examples include the Christian Holy Trinity; the Hindu *Trimurti* of Brahma, Vishnu and Shiva; and the 'three sisters' of the Celtic Triple Goddess. Three wise men identified the infant Jesus as the foretold king. In Ancient Greece there were three lords of the created world: Zeus, Poseidon and Hades. In stories from around the world, three brothers face the same challenge; three successive attempts result in success. The number twelve thus represents the intersection of space and time. In Classical mythology there were twelve seats on Mount Olympus. There are twelve tribes of Israel and the Heavenly Jerusalem has twelve gates. There are twelve calendar months and zodiacal signs; however, there are thirteen lunar months in the year. If twelve is the number of completion, thirteen represents a higher order of learning. In many traditions the master has twelve initiates: Jesus chose twelve disciples and conferred healing powers upon them (*Holy Bible*: Matthew 10:1). The boy in this story is the thirteenth witness to the secret world: he ultimately attains wisdom and hence spiritual authority.

The Hero

1. The hero is revered as the incarnation of all that is best in man. His attractiveness is largely due to his masculine good looks. On the basis of his mighty muscles, he is ascribed moral qualities of bravery and protectiveness. Women are unconsciously drawn to him because of his obvious paternal potential. Infants with a

strong genetic inheritance will have a higher chance of survival. The benefit is mutual: hero-figures can father children on a large number of women without accusations of promiscuity.

This projection of personality is not as irrational as it appears. The hero's reputation for public spirit is based partly on his behaviour. If he wishes to retain popular support, the hero may transgress certain social boundaries but not others. The Greek champion and the modern sports star both find that they are subject to unspoken constraints. The hero may engage in serial monogamy but never in dubious transactions. He may be unfaithful but he must never be dishonest. He should use his force against monstrous adversaries: he must never abuse his strength to dominate those weaker than himself. The hero may be involved in struggles for power, but he must never abuse his gifts to become a tyrant.

The hero-ideal has always been open to manipulation. The Greek philosopher Plato (c.428-348 BC) discusses in his *Republic* what he calls the 'noble lie': the idea that all men are made from earth, but that in a few the earth has been mixed with gold, rendering them inherently superior to their fellow-men and so fit to wield power. This lie, he suggests, is politically useful in that it pre-disposes the mass of people to accept leaders. We long to believe in heroes and saviours who will take responsibility for our fate: a natural elite who are qualified to lead, averting evil and guiding us to victory. The dark aspect of public desire to adulate 'great men' was shown by the ascendancy of Nazi-Aryan supremists before World War II. The forces of group psychology permit the rise to power of tyrants who present a travesty of heroism. The classical heroes journeyed to hell and returned with its secret riches; inappropriately channelled, the same energies can create hell on earth.

2. Changes in the value ascribed to violent force account largely for successive shifts in the role of the hero through the ages. This

reflects a shift in the importance of traditionally masculine activities. In ancient times, wild animals were an important source of food for the tribe. Hunting is a dangerous activity, and depends largely on the willingness of young males to take irrational risks. Whilst they hope to survive, the risk-assessment of young males is impaired under the influence of adrenaline. On an individual level it is not sensible to hazard your life for a meal; from the perspective of the group, it is a perfectly acceptable proposition. A large proportion of the males in a balanced community are numerically expendable. Population replacement rates depend upon the number of offspring per female: only about half the boys need to reach maturity in order for the social unit to reproduce. Those males who survive to maturity start to exhibit considerably less risk-taking behaviour as intellectual assessment replaces instinctive responses.

The Trickster

1. Animal tricksters present a comfortably distant metaphor for the human predicament. Another common trickster-figure is the monkey. Anthropomorphic and agile, he represents the human mind. In the Tibetan Wheel of Life the monkey symbolizes conscious attention which flits from one thing to another in this phenomenal world, like a monkey hopping from branch to branch. The Stone Monkey of Buddhist myth is initially anarchic and arrogant; but after learning his own insignificance, he becomes a savant who conducts the monk Tripitaka (Hsuan Tsang) on his great journey to the West. In Europe, the Trickster is Reynard the Fox who defeats every enemy with his quick wits. His exploits were related by medieval storytellers satirizing contemporary events. Reynard's Globe of Glass was a marvellous treasure which revealed anything that the person consulting it wished to know, but which only ever existed in the imagination of the fox: hence, it signifies a promise which is never delivered.

Reynard's Wonderful Ring is a similar impossibility. Chaucer's *Nun's Priest's Tale (Chanticleer the Cock)* is part of the Reynard tradition.

2. In Tarot, the cards represent different aspect of esoteric wisdom. The major arcane are numbered from 1 (Juggler) to 20 (World); the Fool alone has no number, not being part of the pack. From within the safety of society this tattered figure looks like a tramp, but his staff and cap are gold (the colour of knowledge); the bundle on his stick is white (the colour of secrets and initiation); and his shoes are red (the colour of life). Ignoring the dog pulling at his pants (symbols of animal nature and human possessions), he walks confidently towards the unknown. Like the Hindu *saddhu* or wandering mendicant, his shabby appearance conceals inner wisdom and enlightenment.

3. Habitually self-centred and conniving, the Trickster is also at times a pitiful or even tragic figure. Often his own curiosity or pride prove to be his downfall. His dilemmas represent the conflicting moral and profane aspects of the human psyche. These apparently opposing aspects of his character are not contradictory but complementary. Bringing both order and chaos, the Trickster represents the dual nature of creation. He is frequently credited with creating the world but also with intro-ducing death, usually as the result of some foolish decision. However, death is a necessary part of the life cycle. We must harvest the seeds for next year's sowing; pruning clears the way for spring growth. The Trickster may seem destructive, but he is also a catalyst of change. His antics are the engine which drives existence in this world.

The Wise Man

1. The wise man is often shown leaning on a stick. His wooden

staff is as much for combat as for support. It is also a symbol of his miraculous powers. Whereas the hero traditionally relies on physical prowess, the magus can manipulate the magico-spiritual dimension of life. The magic wand also has obvious phallic symbolism, reminding us that the sage was once a young hero himself. As a token sceptre it recalls his own sacred kingship which the hero is now in a position to supplant.

2. Taoism was founded in the sixth-century BC by the philosopher-sage Lao Tzu, author of the *Tao Te Ch'ing*. According to Taoist doctrine, the aim of humanity is to live in harmony with the forces of heaven and earth. Immortality is an indicator of having achieved this spiritual balance. Over subsequent centuries devotees made the quest for eternal life a key tenet of their faith. Stories of the Eight Immortals indicated that immortality was within the reach of anyone who followed the precepts of Taoism. The Eight Immortals are not, strictly speaking, gods: they are legendary personages who enjoy the Peaches of Immortality at banquets held by the Queen Mother of the West. The octet were not connected until around the fourteenth century at the start of the Ming dynasty, although their stories indicate a much earlier provenance. Some of them reflect the Taoist belief that immortality can be obtained, not only through study and reflection, but by the ingestion of certain substances. The Taoists devised a range of anti-ageing techniques including yoga, meditation and the consumption of 'elixirs' containing mercury or lead. Unsurprisingly, these combinations failed to elicit the desired results.

The Ogre

1. The tramp represents an alternative system of belief, for he is blessed in intangible ways. His lack of possessions leaves him blessedly free of worldly constraints. Unencumbered by respon-

sibility, the tramp can wander when and where he will. His disdain for material wealth may be countered by a rich inner life. This is the way of the *saddhu* (a wandering mendicant) who leaves his home and family in search of spiritual enlightenment. Sometimes the tramp becomes a holy man, able to confer blessings and heal the sick. He may eventually be revealed as a king in disguise and return to his realm bearing the boon of insight. Through suffering long privations, the tramp can become privy to esoteric knowledge. In this guise he is also an aspect of the older Trickster, the holder of hidden wisdom with the potential for both destruction and creation.

2. The tale of the Troll King can be interpreted in psychoanalytic terms as a description of child development. The entrance to the cave recalls another passageway which the infant can never re-enter. The troll king represents the all-powerful father figure whom the child both respects and fears. The maid is a grotesque travesty of the mother, both protecting and restraining the child. The wild dance articulates emotional desires, freed from the restraints of conscious inhibition. The stolen jewels represent the wisdom of the unconscious mind. The treasures of the under-world appear worthless in the bright light of day; but what could be more valuable than coal, which can warm the house on a winter's night?

If you want to know how trolls dance, listen to the last movement of *Peer Gynt (Suite One)* by the Norwegian composer Edvard Grieg. This evocative piece of music was written to accompany Ibsen's 'dramatic poem' based on the exploits of this legendary character.

Archetypal Stories

1. It is sometimes said that there are only seven basic plots, and all stories are a reworking of these themes. They are listed by

Booker (2004) as Rags to Riches; The Hero's Quest; Voyage and Return; Overcoming the Monster; Tragedy; Comedy, and Rebirth. All books, plays and films arguably take one of these basic themes and rework it in some way. Thus, *Pride and Prejudice* or *Pretty Woman* are variants of Cinderella, or 'Rags to Riches'. The power of these universal themes and concerns is evident in the survival of traditional stories. Great writers such as Tolkien or Ursula Le Guin incorporate potent mythic forms and archetypal figures in their work. They are wise to do so: re-workings of old stories such as the Arthurian legends, which have achieved a psychically near-optimum form over centuries of transmission, are likely to be more effective than 'original' science fiction.

In terms of structure, the variety of basic plots is possibly even smaller than seven. The best stories begin with either 'He set out on a journey' or 'A stranger came to town', with either positive or negative consequences ensuing. (Children's books sometimes preface this with, 'Their parents went on holiday'). It is this change in the world order which precipitates the possibility of adventure. On a deeper level, most life stories contain elements of all the great narrative themes. Our scripts often feature similar episodes although they may be inverted or occur in a different order. Shared experiences across time and culture define our common humanity. From a spiritual perspective, we all have the same lessons to learn.

Creation and Re-creation

1. Many traditions hold that this world is only one of many. Hindu cosmology relates that Maya, the manifest world, is only a dream in the mind of Brahma. When Brahma awakes each day, a universe comes into being; when he falls asleep again many millennia later, that universe ceases to be. We are now deep into Kali Yoga, the Age of Iron, and may expect to sleep soon. It is therefore unwise to become too attached to material things, for

by their very nature they can give only temporary satisfaction. The Aztec people of Central America believed that this world was the fifth attempt at creation, each of the previous ones having been destroyed by a cataclysm: this gave urgency to the demands of the sun for fresh blood to help him on his daily journey across the sky. The sense that we are only here temporarily and on sufferance has modern parallels in the ecological movement. People behave differently depending on whether they think that they have a right to exploit natural resources, or that they are only custodians of this planet.

2. The story of Atrahasis ('Extra-wise') was first told in Ancient Sumeria. The version here is based on tablets preserved in the library of King Ashurbanipal of Nineveh. A similar story is found in the Babylonian epic of Gilgamesh the Hero. In this version, the survivor is called Ut-napishtim ('He found life'); after the rains cease he lets loose a dove, a swallow and a raven to search for dry land. This story would have been known to the Jewish priests who wrote down the story of Noah and his Ark, for the Jewish people were taken captive by King Nebuchadnezzar in 597BC and held captive in Babylon for sixty years.

Part III: Personal Mythology

1. Howard Thurman, quoted by Myss (2001).

2. Myths which relate the deeds of gods and heroes may be difficult for us to identify with. By contrast folk-tales, which feature ordinary people, are more likely to inspire emulation and so promote psychic integration. This is especially true for children, for whom stories are an important source of release and reassurance. A 'wicked stepmother' is clearly alien: the child is free to resent her without the danger of antagonizing the 'good'

real mother on whom he actually depends. Snow White needs to achieve both independence and mature judgement before she is ready to form an intimate adult relationship. Fairy-tales thus work, both consciously and unconsciously, to support and free the child (Bettelheim 1976). The differentiation between story types is actually somewhat spurious. In traditional societies, sacred stories may be differentiated from folk tales in terms of their overt source and purpose, but both continue to be re-told for similar reasons. They are a source of indirect experiences which have significance for the audience, and inspire the listener to reflect and to act.

3. Which comes first, character or story? Sometimes it is not clear whether character or circumstance determines the course of events. In both life and literature this raises issues of personal responsibility. Homer's *Iliad* frequently portrays his heroes as mere playthings of the Gods, but at other times he implies that their actions do matter. Novelists sometimes portray their characters as victims of circumstance – Hardy's Tess is powerless over her assailant; others imply that individuals have the power to make a difference - in Tolstoy's *Anna Karenina* it is personal decisions determine the course of events. Great stories weave these two elements seamlessly together to create a sense of inevitability which bypasses the debate between free will and fate.

A similar debate applies to the construction of a life story. Archetypes are psychic forms which manifest pre-natally and cross-culturally. As the primary presence, they could be argued to determine the selection of story line. In one sense they precede the development of a personal narrative template derived from life experience. However, the tendency to perceive pattern and create stories is also an innate product of the human mind. Narrative construction occurs in parallel with the allocation of roles in the development of your personal mythology.

4. The two constituent components in the development of personal mythology are narrative script and archetypal form. People with a dominant visual-spatial processing style tend to conceive their personal mythology primarily in pictorial terms, although still retaining the narrative element. There is a tradition in Indian art where several episodes from an epic – involving the same characters – can be portrayed within a single picture frame. Other visual parallels for the process of constructing a personal mythology are the mosaic picture or patchwork quilt. These can include both old and new elements artfully incorporated into an original design.

5. For the visual-spatial processor, it is the archetypal figures which feature most significantly in their life story. They attach proportionately less importance to the identity of the individuals who actually fill those roles. This is an attitude more common in men, who are sometimes accused of treating women as stereotypical figures devoid of feelings. Males do have a greater incidence of visual-spatial processing, reflected in the fact that the majority of great artists and scientists over the past few centuries have been men. However, there are also many women for whom conventional female roles form a cornerstone of their adult identity. A wife's affection for her husband may be based partly on his ability to play his part in the marital contract. So long as both parties agree on the assumptions underlying their relationship, this is not an issue. Problems often only arise when our life circumstances change. One partner losing their job, or the arrival of children, can disrupt the balance of what was previously a mutually satisfactory arrangement.

6. When modifying your personal mythology, it is important to differentiate between formative experience and destructive patterns. Often the most difficult times of our life have made us stronger and more insightful. The understanding and resilience

which we gain from these episodes can be used to help others and make the world a better place. Your life is like a novel: you cannot only read the chapters where good things happen. Some people thrive on danger, and actively seek out challenging situations. Others simply reinforce negative experiences by repeatedly re-enacting events. Such patterns of behaviour require a conscious change of script, characters or even setting. This process is initially daunting but potentially fulfilling. Developing your personal mythology is the ultimate act of creation. In taking responsibility for our own stories, we gain a sense of purpose in life.

7. The Ancient Greeks had a concept which they called *eudaimonia*. This is often translated as 'happiness'. A more accurate definition is something along the lines of 'feelings accompanying behaviour consistent with your daimon'. Your daimon is your spirit or true self, a state of excellence which gives meaning and direction to your life. Eudaimonia is a state in which you are being true to yourself. You are striving to realize your potential and thereby living the most fulfilling life possible. When you look back on your life or tell others your story, you try to make it congruent with this inner self which is the 'real' you. This sense of being true to your inner calling or life purpose is what Hillman (1996) calls the 'acorn theory' and Myss (2001) describes as honouring your 'sacred contract'. When you are acting in accordance with your true self, you experience the state of 'living in the moment' which has been called flow (Csikszentmihalyi 1991).

Exercises & Appendices

The disciple once complained,
"You tell us stories, but you never
reveal their meaning to us."
Said the master,
"How would you like it if someone
offered you fruit and masticated it
before giving it to you?"
(Anthony de Mello, 1981)

Exercise A:
Encountering Archetypal Figures

You have met the twelve major archetypal figures many times before. In this exercise, try to recall where you have encountered them in your own life. For each archetype write down:

a) What are the characteristic features of this figure? List the ones that seem most important to you.

b) What examples of this archetype can you think of? Think of books you have read; films or plays you have seen; contemporary public or political figures, and so on.

c) What does this figure mean to you personally? Think of people in your own life who have these characteristics.

Princess

Clever girl

Great Mother

Bad Mother

Grandmother

Wicked Witch

Infant Prince

Urchin

Hero

Trickster

Wise Old Man

Ogre / Tramp

Further Thoughts

Exercise B:
Identifying Life Themes

You encounter story sequences in many forms: fairy tales, novels, films, plays and memoirs. These are all sources of material for the development of your own narrative template. Many of the elements of your script come from stories which have influenced you, especially in early life. If you study these stories, you will identify some recurring features. Young children like to hear the same tales told over and over again. As you become older, you are able to assimilate more information from the first encounter. Only a few books actually improve on closer study. A 'classic' is a book which benefits from being re-read, because you can appreciate it from different perspectives as your own life-experience increases.

Some stories you may feel naturally drawn to: they seem to reflect a deep underlying truth about the world. These are the narratives which will inform your life script. Other work you might appreciate in a more intellectual way: the construction of the scene, or the cleverness of the plot. This may stay in your memory, but it will not become a part of your personal script.

Study the questions below. They will help you to identify your dominant life themes.

1.   What is your favourite fairy tale?

2.   What was your favourite book as a child?

3.   What did you like about this book?

4.   What is your favourite book right now?

5.   What do you like or admire about this book?

6.   What are your five top films of all time? What do they have in common?

7.   What poems do you know by heart? When and why did you learn them?

8.   What sort of songs do you enjoy? Do you know the words and sing along?

9.   What is your favourite quotation, saying or motto?

Looking in particular at your answers to questions 2 and 4:

10. In what ways did and does your own life reflect, or contrast with, the experiences of the main character? With other characters? Are you happy with this identification (or contrast)? Why (or why not)? What would you like to do about this?

Exercise C:
Working With Images

A picture speaks a thousand words and seeing is believing. The media are well aware of the potential of pictures to shape our perceptions. We can use the power of imagework to change our understanding of the world. Through visualization we can modify the archetypal figures in our minds. Imagework is a practical tool with which we can alter our life scripts. Visualization is also a way to clarify and concentrate on what we hope will come to pass. Whatever we create in the world, from an omelette to a love affair, begins as an image in our minds. This is similar to the same way in which prayer works: by focusing on what we wish for, we help to bring it to realization.

The first exercise will help you deal with someone with whom you are having problems. The second addresses issues of personal development. You will invite an image that draws on the power of the subconscious to formulate the problem more effectively. By working with a mental image, you can address the issue in ways that might seem too difficult in real life. Amazingly, the insights you attain will actually help you to operate more effectively.

Before doing these exercises, read through the instructions carefully. You may like to record them and play them back to guide you during the session. Alternatively, you could ask a trusted friend to sit with you and read them out. Wear loose warm clothes, and perhaps have a blanket to hand. If you are worried that you may forget something, have a notebook beside you: anything important that occurs can be written down to deal with later.

Managing Relationships

Find a quiet place where you can relax without being disturbed. Make sure you are comfortable and your body is well supported. For this exercise you may like to place two chairs opposite one another. The seat in which you are sitting is your position; the opposite one represents the other person with whom you need to engage. Relax and breathe deeply, focusing on the outward breath. Focus on each limb in turn: notice any tension and let it go. Soften your shoulders; your neck; your face. If you feel worried or afraid, let the feeling gather in your stomach and blow it gently out, like fog. If any thoughts come into your mind, simply observe them and let them go. Sense the clean empty space inside your head.

When you are ready, invite a figure into your mind. This figure represents the person with whom you are having problems. Examine this image carefully. What is it wearing? What is it holding? What does this symbolize? Can you walk around and see it from the other side? If not, why not? What does this image tell you about the person it represents? What archetypal figure does it resemble or recall? What associations, both positive and negative, do you have with this archetype?

Now you are going to explore this image-figure more closely. You are going to become this person. It may be helpful to physically move to the other seat. In your mind, enter into the figure. Now you can see things from that point of view. What are you thinking? What are you feeling? Is there anything you want to say? What do you want to explain and justify? How does your original self look from this position? Is there anything about yourself which you can learn?

Take your time and engage fully with this encounter. If you are listening to a tape, pause it now until you are ready to continue.

Come back out of the image-figure and return to your original position. Look at the image again. How do you feel about it now? What have you learnt about the figure that could help you? Is there anything you want to say to them? If you speak to the figure, listen to its reply. Perhaps you notice changes in the image. What other ways could you deal with it, knowing what you know now?

Repeat this switching of roles again if you feel it would be helpful.

When you are ready, thank the figure for appearing and say farewell. Slowly come back to the room. The image may still be very clear in your mind. Give your thoughts time to clear and let any strong emotions subside. You may want to have a drink or eat something.

Being and Becoming

Find a quiet place where you can relax without being disturbed. You may want to lie down. Make sure you are warm and comfortable. Relax and breathe deeply, focusing on the sensation of air in your nostrils. Roll your eyes upwards and as you release them, count down from five to nought. Focus on each limb in turn: notice any tension and release it. As your body relaxes, sense yourself drifting gently upwards. Feel yourself floating just above the ground. If any thoughts come into your mind, simply observe them and let them go. As you breathe out, imagine that you are blowing them out of your brain like dusty cobwebs. Sense the bright empty space inside your head.

When you are ready, invite an image into your mind. This image represents yourself as you are now. Accept the first image which arises, no matter how unlikely it may appear. This image is a gift from your subconscious, and represents a holistic picture of yourself. It may be a figure; or an animal; or a plant. The image will probably be a picture, but it may manifest as a sound or smell. If you are having trouble perceiving anything, ask yourself whether an image arose which you initially rejected. If there is still nothing, accept the emptiness and work with that.

Look at this image-self carefully. It reflects the way you perceive yourself. How do you look? How do you move? If the image is a figure, what are you wearing? What are you holding? What might this symbolize? What archetypal figure does your image remind you of? How do you feel about this image?

Be kind to your image-self: it may have important things to tell you.

When you are ready, thank the image and let it dissolve. Now you are going to invite another image into your mind. This image represents what you would like to be. It may be a person; a bird or animal; a flower or tree. This time, you have some control over the image that appears.

Greet the new image and study it carefully. What does it look like? What does it represent for you? In what ways are you already like this image? Now you are going to become this image. In your mind, enter into the image. How does it feel to be this image? What are you thinking? What are you doing? How did you come to be this way?

Take your time and engage fully with this encounter. If you are listening to a tape, pause it now until you are ready to continue.

Identify fully with your new image. This is the person that you have decided to become. The image represents your future self. You might like to make some small sign, such as touching your cheek, which will help you remember how it felt to be this person. This sign can be used to summon the power of the image whenever you need it. A simple word used as a mantra can have the same effect.

When you are ready, thank the image for appearing and bid it farewell. Start to count up from one to five as you come back to the room. Open your eyes slowly. Give your mind time to clear before doing anything else. You may want to have a drink or eat something.

When you need to remind yourself of your new image, make your secret sign or say your special word quietly to yourself. This will remind yourself of how it feels to think and act in the way you have visualized.

Exercise D:
Developing Your Script

You already have a life script. You have been carefully constructing it since earliest childhood, using a variety of sources to compose the plot and cast the characters. Once you become consciously aware of this process, there may be aspects which you would like to change. When you decide to work on your personal mythology it can be helpful to write down your thoughts and plans. If you identify the main characters in your life, you will become aware of the roles which you yourself are playing. True friends are those with whom you feel most fully yourself: with them there is no sense of acting, for they perceive you as the person whom you want to be. Other people in your environment may pull you down, making you feel somehow dissatisfied with yourself. You are probably caught in a repetitive pattern of mutual self-denial: this will not help them either, so it might be best to reduce the contact you have with them. Never forget, however, that you drew them into your life for a reason (whether consciously or otherwise): sometimes those who irritate us most are those from whom we have most to learn. There will be still other characters who you would like to be a part of your life story: consider ways in which you could attract those individuals (or others who might play a comparable role) into your life.

As you complete this section, try to be as truthful with yourself as possible. Be specific about what you would like to achieve. Write your answers down in full so that you can consider them properly. Use further pages as necessary: a loose-leaf notebook can be helpful.

A. People In My Life

Who are the most important people in my life at present?
For each person:
- Is this person's effect on me positive or negative? In what ways?
- What archetypal features can I see in this person as they relate to me?

What other characters would I like to have in my life-story?
For each character:
- Who do I know who might already be playing a similar role?
- What archetypal figure might this person represent to me?
- How could I develop this relationship more fully?
- Where might I find someone else to fill this role?
- How would this friendship benefit me?
- What could I offer to help and attract them?

B. Writing a Life Script

The Story So Far

What are the most important events in my life to date?
For each incident:
- How did I feel about this event at the time?
- Was the overall effect positive or negative?
- Have similar things happened to me before or afterwards?
- Can I identify a pattern here? (Even chaos is a pattern!)

What I Will Do Next

What experiences do I want to have in my life story?
Today or tomorrow:
- What do I want to do or achieve?
- What can I do to make this happen?
- What might stop me? How can I prevent this?
- Is there an alternative that would satisfy me?
- What am I going to do now?

Within a month:
- What do I want to do or achieve?
- What can I do to make this happen?
- What might stop me? How can I prevent this?
- Is there an alternative that would satisfy me?
- What am I going to do now?

By this time next year:
- What do I want to do or achieve?
- What can I do to make this happen?
- What might stop me? How can I prevent this?
- Is there an alternative that would satisfy me?
- What am I going to do now?

Within ten years (or, before I die):
- What do I want to do or achieve?
- What can I do to make this happen?
- What might stop me? How can I prevent this?
- Is there an alternative that would satisfy me?
- What am I going to do now?

Remember: Your life script is your personal story. Creating and casting it is your most important work. May your path be smooth, your blanket warm and your waterbottle always full.

Exercise E:
Constructing a Life Collage

Now you have identified the things you want in your life. A life collage is a practical visual reminder of your goals.

For this exercise you will be working with pictures. Get a selection of magazines – around ten different ones which you will not mind cutting up. Some of them should relate to your current interests; others to activities which you have never tried – sailing, photography or needlework. Choose a wide range of subjects, from popular science to celebrity gossip. You can also use photographs of yourself and people that you know.

Get a large piece of card (A1 size) or a cork notice-board. You will also need sticky tape or glue. Find a space where you can spread out your work for an hour or two without being disturbed.

Go through your magazines, cutting out pictures that appeal to you. Tear out any slogans or headlines that catch your attention too. Try to find images that represent the important people in your world. These may be actual people, or figures who you want to include in your life. Make sure that you have at least one image for each major archetype.

Arrange the pictures on your board: cut them in various shapes, and stick them at different angles. Add quotes or slogans that enhance the meaning of the images. Decorate them with coloured crayons or a fancy border. Your collage shows your world the way you want it to be. Be as crazy and artistic as you like: the life that you envisage should include some fun!

Put your collage up somewhere you can see it every day. Perhaps you could hang it in your kitchen, close to where you sit for breakfast. Each morning look at your collage and focus on the images. By regularly visualizing your ideal world, you help it to manifest in reality.

Appendix A:
The Role of Myth

Myth is as old as mankind. Ever since people became aware of themselves as individuals, they have wondered what it means to be human. We contemplate the great mysteries of existence: Who am I? Where do I come from? What is the purpose of life? Stories are one way to explore these existential questions. Once our basic needs for food and shelter have been met, we start to look for a purpose in life. Individually and collectively, we try to construct a world view which gives meaning to our existence. These sacred stories have survived because they address universal concerns and convey fundamental truths about life.

The word 'mythology' originates in Ancient Greece. *Mythos* literally means 'utterance' or 'what is spoken', from the Indo-European root *mu*, to mutter or murmur. *Logos* means 'word' in the sense of a reasoned discourse or doctrine. In the fifth century BC a myth was simply a narrative of events. At this point the term had no connotation of fantasy or fabrication. The great historian Herodotus (c.484-420BC), in his account of the war between the Greeks and Persians, recorded all the facts which he could gather and left it to his audience to determine what was true and what was not. Plato (c.428-348BC) tried to differentiate legends from historical events, but this was for ethical reasons. He disapproved of the stories related by Homer in the *Iliad* because they showed the gods engaging in immoral behaviour. This did not concern the majority of the population, who viewed the deities as existing above social conventions. Their behaviour might provide a good example or a terrible warning, but they were above the ordinary concerns of everyday life. The Greek philosopher Aristotle (384-322BC) analyzed the cathartic function of tragic plays: experiencing intense feelings of pity and fear leaves us feeling emotionally cleansed. Conversely, tales of heroes overcoming monsters can inspire and arouse us. Such dramatic effects mattered far more than the literal truth of the tales. For the Ancient Greeks the historical accuracy of these stories was not important. Their myths provided the patterns by which they knew themselves as a people. Whether or not the stories were factually 'true' was of secondary concern.

Stories are always popular; the reasons we tell them are as varied as the tales themselves. Myths are a special category of story and fulfil some specific functions.

Firstly, a myth must entertain us. Since earliest times, people have told tales to amuse their listeners and to pass the time. Unless a story captures our imagination we will not want to repeat it again. The old mythmakers knew that they must win their audience: early bards developed tricks of the trade to aid memory and engage attention, such as the 'rule of threes' (there are three brothers; the hero answers three questions; he succeeds on the third attempt). Myths adhere to a strictly evolutionary code of survival: only the best stories survive to replicate for the next generation of listeners.

Secondly, a myth may be told to explain something. Myths provide us with possible answers to profound questions: Who made the world? Why is there night and day? Why does evil exist? What happens to people when they die? Myth presents a cosmology, or model of the universe, compatible with the knowledge of the prevailing culture. This image of reality is shaped by historical experience and geographical environment. Myths address the preoccupations and concerns of the people who formulate and listen to them. The stories which seem most relevant to us are those which reflect our own circumstances. For people in rural communities, stories about nature reflected their interests and experience. When we hear thunder, the gods and giants are fighting; the rainbow is a bridge from heaven to earth; earthquakes are the stirrings of a sleeping monster; that volcano is a dragon's fiery lair.

Some myths contain codified references to natural forces, but they are far more than primitive explanations of the universe. Their allusions operate at a deeper level of comprehension. The ice giants represent the threat posed by freezing Nordic winters. The slaying of Humbaba censors the destruction of cedar forests by Sumerian raiders. Medusa literally petrifies those who would deny the power of the feminine. Myths are stories which operate on many different levels simultaneously. Disguised as folktales, they address both practical and philosophical issues. It is this ambivalence which accounts for their lasting appeal. Even if we no longer have to fight dragons, we are still surrounded by metaphorical monsters.

Myths may also explain cultural customs and justify social conditions. Traditional tales provide us with a formal manifesto of group values and beliefs. Old stories address moral issues such as the legitimacy of the prevailing distribution of resources. The social hierarchy of Scandinavia exists because the god Heimdall once walked the earth and received different levels of hospitality from various couples, whom he rewarded with appropriate children. Some people are lords and warriors whilst others are serfs: this was determined by our forefathers' behaviour. Men are more powerful than women because originally the gods made only men in their image. Pandora was sent to punish mankind for the theft of fire and she brought a box full of troubles. Myths transmit the morals, ethics and beliefs of past times to future generations, ensuring that the individual can integrate with society. They provide a social charter which both explains and reconciles our lot.

Thirdly, a myth may be told to educate an audience. Stories are a good way to teach by stealth, especially to children. Through myth the accumulated wisdom of a people is codified and passed on. Fire coals can be carried safely in a clay pot. Dangerous animals may lurk beside the river. The deer will pass through after the autumn leaves to turn gold. Other messages may be more profound and operate at a deeper level. It is both generous and judicious to give hospitality to travellers. It is dangerous to marry outside your community lest your wife turns out to be a witch. Do not lust after your mother: genetic research reinforces the universal incest taboo. Great risks are necessary to obtain great rewards; but if you challenge the status quo you may bring destruction upon those dearest to you.

Sometimes the instructional purpose is more explicit. Dramatic stories are more likely to be remembered than a dry list of facts. It is hard to recall a series of unrelated objects, but if we can make connections they are easy to remember. Narrative forms a mnemonic device encoding information for future use. Tales of the Hawaiian goddess Pele relate the sequence of events to be expected in a volcanic eruption, preserving the experience of former generations. The 'song-lines' of the Australian Aboriginal people provide a mental map of the geographical features and resources which are encountered on significant journeys. Structuring elements into a story sequence enables people to remember them over long periods of time and recall them accurately when they are needed.

Finally, myths are a source of spiritual enlightenment. They deal with profound issues, providing both inspiration and consolation. They seek ways to explain and justify the human condition. They offer us reassurance that our lives are not meaningless and that our individual existence is part of a larger pattern. Sacred stories contain spiritual truths which resonate with the human heart. They weave fact with fantasy to convey the universal psychological reality of the characters and events described. Myths relate the events of a timeless past and so set a precedent for the present and future. They portray a timeless reality which raises us above the limitations of the human condition.

Myths are traditional stories that address universal existential concerns. They may explain things, but they are not scientific analyses nor philosophical discourses. Myths contain magic and metamorphosis; they are not intended to be taken as literal descriptions of everyday life. The embellishments are there partly to make the story more interesting. They also serve to expand the incidents from the particular to the universal. Myths use symbol and metaphor to communicate directly with the human psyche. They are a way of reconciling us with the unjust and brutal aspects of existence whilst simultaneously celebrating the beauty of creation. Stories help us to find pattern and meaning in our lives. Through myth we can learn to know ourselves, understand the origin of our being and the features of our world, and start to chart our own destinies.

Appendix B:
Travelling Tales

'Archetypal' myths recur in cultures around the world. The Creation, the Flood and the Hero's Quest are the best known examples. The themes of these stories reflect universal concerns and they speak to the audience on a variety of levels. They may recall folk memories of actual historical events; explain natural phenomena; or function as a call to action, invoking the spiritual development of the listener. Some mythologists say that the widespread occurrence of many mythic themes is simply the product of cultural diffusion. Their distribution reflects the ancient transmission of stories, either carried outwards as mankind migrated from his original homelands or related by travelling bards in the days before satellite television made news simultaneously available around the world. Myths pass easily from one language to another because their content is more important than their form. Others argue that such stories differ in enough details to indicate that they developed independently. According to this view, the spontaneous but separate evolution of similar stories (polygenesis) reveals the innate structure of the human psyche. The widespread occurrence of motifs such as the Flood reflects the fundamental preoccupations of humankind.

Polygenesis and diffusion are not necessarily conflicting explanations: the two processes may operate in parallel. A story may have been invented independently, but in retelling it the narrator may incorporate elements from a tale he has encountered elsewhere. Each storyteller tries to make their tales relevant, memorable and interesting. In some cultures and epochs, there may be an emphasis on retelling the myth in a highly stylized and conventional form. In others, embroidery and elaboration may be more highly valued as evidence of the bard's skill. Elaboration makes it more likely that events and characters from other sources will be incorporated into the original story. In this way, tales of outstanding deeds tend to accrete around significant characters. Heroes such as Herakles are credited with far more adventures that are possible in a single life-time. Diverse stories may also be linked as a form of mnemonic. The listing of Greek heroes who sailed with Jason and the Argonauts makes it easier to recall their separate attributes and deeds.

In an oral tradition, there is no pure and original version of the myth. The authenticity of the tale is not important: the point of interest is that the stories have survived. Myths only persist because they speak to the narrator and the listener: they address real concerns, and they resonate within the soul. As stories travel, their protagonists acquire features in line with local cultural norms. In practical terms, the characters are socially assimilated so that they become acceptable to the new audience. The arche-types who speak through myth are alive and well in the world today. The Goddess still walks among us, although she may be hard to recognize at first sight. Her old ways have been modified to suit modern manners; her dress will change with the fashions; she may even use her married name. Her consort's face may vary, but his behaviour gives him away. In the people around us we can recognize all the characters from the old stories.

It is interesting that in cultures without a high artistic tradition, only major distinguishing physical characteristics of the gods were given. The delineation of detailed features was left to the imagination of each worshipper. In Viking mythology, for example, we hear of Thor's red hair or Odin's one eye; but the details of description are passed over by the narrator. In this way, the gods can take on the faces and personal characteristics of the people who have passed through our lives. They become more plausible and consequently real for us. The same is true for folk-tales, which by their nature are not associated with a high artistic tradition. We know very little about the appearance of our fairy-tale heroines, apart from distinguishing features like the colour of Goldilocks' hair. Paradoxically, less is more: the absence of information enables us to identify with the characters. In the absence of visual images, it is easier to personalize the story and thus perceive its relevance to our own life. In this aspect, literature is closer than film to the tradition of the storyteller.

Appendix C:
Learning Styles

We learn by processing information gained through our senses about the external world. The most dominant sense is sight: around 80% of our sensory data is derived from visual sources. In modern society this includes written words, which may be in the form of text or slogans. Different information is gained through the other senses, predominantly hearing and touch. For certain specific tasks, such as identifying foods which are safe to eat, taste and smell become more important. This raw sensory data is combined with knowledge from memory in our analysis of the world.

'Learning styles' relate to those parts of the brain which are most active when we are receiving and processing information. The right hemisphere of the brain deals predominantly with visual and spatial information received in the form of images. People in whom the right hemisphere is most active are said to have a visual-spatial learning style. The left hemisphere deals with information received aurally and sequentially. This includes structured series of sound, such as spoken sentences, which we perceive as 'making sense'. If you prefer to get information from words rather than images, you are said to have a verbal-sequential learning style. The written word is an anomalous case in that it provides aural information coded in a visual (symbolic) form. Cognitive studies have shown that the brain converts written words into their spoken equivalent and proceeds to process them as aural information.

The structure of the brain gives an interesting twist to this process. Nerve fibres carrying information received from the sensory organs cross over at a junction called the corpus callosum in the centre of the brain. Consequently the left hemisphere of the brain receives information for processing from the right side of the body, whilst the right hemisphere receives data from the left side. If someone receives an injury to the left side of their head, it is the right-hand side of their body which may be affected. In modern society most information is given and received in a logical-sequential way which favours left-hemisphere processing. Consequently in the majority of people the left hemisphere is dominant, as evinced in the fact that most people are right-handed. Notably, great artists and sportsmen who have superior visual-spatial skills are disproportionately left-handed.

Students with a verbal-sequential learning style find it easiest to learn things when they can follow the underlying logical structure. People with a visual-spatial style prefer to receive data in a more holistic manner. Boys are more likely to be visual processors, which has both advantages and drawbacks. When learning they will find diagrams and 'mind maps' more helpful than pages of text; if written notes are provided they need to structure them with highlighted headings and bullet-point lists. In extreme cases they may be diagnosed as dyslexic and need help with study skills. However, visualizers have an overview approach which enables them to see the connections between individual concepts or events. They are more likely to study art or music than literature or history; but those who persevere with science or mathematics are often the most brilliantly gifted.

Acknowledgements

This book is dedicated to Annapurna, Wulfie and Kyrian for all they have taught me.

Many people have provided support and inspiration for this book. The contributions are too many to list, but I am eternally grateful to all the friends and students whose stories have cast light on my own. Their time and company have made this path a rewarding one. In particular, I am thankful for Kathy Thexton, for her generosity and hospitality; Lucinda Evans, for her personal integrity and practical expertise; and Jessica Burnett-Stuart, for her sincerity and insight.

Thanks to the Broomfield Class of 2008, especially Moira Murdoch and Diane Lockett, for all the coffee; Rachel Kent, for more champagne; Sally Durant, for social ethos; Louise Selby, for liberal loans; Heidi Lewis, for introducing me to the artist's way; Rasha Hagras, for integrity; Shahana Baig, for her story; and Susan Ross, Antonia Hastings, Keren Tweeddale and Justine Setchell for comparisons and contrasts. From the same vintage, thanks to Amanda Moore, for feeding the boys; Catherine Cowen, for always seeing the bright side; and Beth van der Eems, for the music. I am grateful to Rita Kamat, for community spirit; Ruth Gledhill, for ecumenical insight; Elaine Bancroft and Bet York, for deep thought; Alidz Pambakian, for providing cover; Susie Byers, for having belief; Marj Davie, for positive outlook; and Sonia Wykes, Heather Ketel, Helen Batten and the rest of my 'colleagues' for endless functional help.

Thanks also to Brian Rogers & Nicki Rowlings, for living the life; Jane Thornback & Hugh Bagnall-Oakeley, for good practice; Sue O'Rourke, for constant recollection; Vicky Peirson, for shared laughter; Mandi White, for her sense of style; Kathy Stevens, for her values; Beth Simmons, for sporting support; Simone

Ackermans, for a once-upon-a-time suggestion; Judith Moore, for all the jokes; Julie Branch, for choosing the scenic route; Anne Peacock, for analogous anecdotes; Rose Constantine, for faith; Angela Pickup, for perseverance; Deborah Curle, for philosophical philandering; Deena Fishbein, for another story; Laura Newry, for a quote; Clare Batten, for a conversation; Bill Byrne, for tortoise tips; Antonella Harrison, for the dancing; Emma Heard, for the singing; Kathryn Ellis, for affirmative attitude; and Lorraine Wicks and Fran Fell, for artistic inspiration. Olivia Stewart, Emily Kerr, Kerstin Stein, Vanessa Gilbert, Vicky Raymond and Nadhini da Silva have shared complementary experiences. My Book Club – Carol Swetenham, Margaret Panayi, Cathy James, Alison Fullerton, Aleka Loizou and Fiona Smith – have been a staple source of high life and low culture.

From further afield and longer ago, thanks to Kathryn (Adams), Lorraine Martin and Sue Hand for safekeeping memories of early days; also to Mary Forty, Clare Glasspool and Jane ('C') Welsh, Queen's College contemporaries and co-conspirators. Salutations to Gerry Hackett, for confounding expectations. Affectionate thanks to Mike Jones, whose faith first instilled confidence. Ciao to Mike Atkin, for positive paradigm. Thanks also to Angela (Bainton) Mathieson, Angela (Kelly) Brosnan, Mala Saye, Ruth Saunders, George Davey Smith, Dave Hamill, Mike Bury and many others for sharing in the narrative.

My students have been a constant source of illumination: special mention must be made of Elisabeth Gick, Elizabeth Bell, Sally Hunkin, Carole Tucker, Lucinda Bolton, Jacki Blanchfield, Martin Johnson, Tom Whyte and Alvin Robins for their contributions to classes.

In both their personal and professional capacities, I am grateful to John Dinwoodie, for metaphysical metaphors; Charlotte Suthrell, for original perspectives; Karen Iredale, for creative collaboration; Sara Bailey, for story trajectory; John Kent, for voice dialogue; Mary Medlicott and Hilary Watkins, for narrative devices; Pat Rabbit and Alfred Gell, for academic inspiration; Steve Batchelor, Elaine Petruccetti and Alison Granger, for teaching tips; Jurgen Wolff, for brainstorming; Florence Hughes and Andrew Lawson, for technical information; Vibeke Dahl, for the photograph; Mike Thexton, for editorial expertise; Julian Robbins and Owen Burnham, for extra assistance; Stuart Davies and Nick Welch, for production processes; Wendy Lazear and Catherine Clarke, for literary midwifery; and Mark Brighton at Kew Bookshop, for bibliographic advice. Special thanks to my agent, Susan Mears, who has sustained me with both wisdom and joy.

My family – in particular Margie Hall and Rachel Bayly – have provided emotional succour over the years. Kathleen Regan has been a stellar in-law. Thanks to Alison, Ginny and especially Lucy, for constant affection and sisterly support. My parents, John and Liz, told me the first stories. Beyond all, Peter's presence has helped me make this journey.

Bibliography

Armstrong, Karen. *A Short History of Myth.* Edinburgh: Cannongate Books (2005).

Berne, Eric. *What Do You Say After You Say Hello?* London: Andrew Deutsch (1974).

Bettelheim, Bruno. *The Uses of Enchantment.* England: Thames & Hudson (1976).

Bolen, Jean Shinoda. *Goddesses in Everywoman.* New York: Harper & Row (1984).

Booker, Christopher. *The Seven Basic Plots.* New York: Continuum Books (2004).

Burkhard, Gudrun. *Taking Charge: Your Life Patterns and Their Meaning.* 1st ed 1992.

London: Floris Books (1997).

Cameron, Julia. *The Artist's Way.* London: Souvenir Press (1994).

Campbell, Joseph. *The Hero With A Thousand Faces.* NJ: Princeton University Press (1949).

Campbell, Joseph. *The Masks of God (Volumes 1-4).* New York: The Viking Press (1959-1968).

Campbell, Joseph. *Myths To Live By.* New York: The Viking Press (1972).

Campbell, Joseph. *The Power of Myth: Interviews with Bill Moyers.* New York: Doubleday (1988).

Cashford, Jules. *The Moon: Myth and Image.* London: Octopus Publishing Group / Cassell (2003).

Csikszentmihalyi, Mihaly. *Flow: The Psychology of Optimal Experience.* New York: Harper Collins (1990).

Eisenberg, D. et al. *Dopamine receptor genetic polymorphisms and body composition in undernourished pastoralists.* BMC Evolutionary Biology 8:173 (2008).

Estes, Clarissa Pinkola. *Women Who Run With The Wolves.* London: Ebury Press / Rider (1992).

Feinstein, D. & Krippner, S. *Personal Mythology*. London: Unwin Hyman (1988).

Frazer, J.G. *The Golden Bough: A Study in Magic and Religion*. 1st edition (2 volumes) (1890); 2nd edition (3 volumes) London: MacMillan (1922).

Glouberman, Dina. *Life Choices, Life Changes*. London: Unwin Hyman (1989).

Gould, Joan. *Spinning Straw into Gold: What Fairy Tales Reveal About the Transformations in a Woman's Life*. New York: Random House (2005).

Green, Liz & Sharman-Burke, Julie. *The Mythic Journey*. London: Eddison Sadd (2000).

Graves, Robert. *The White Goddess*. London: Pelican Books (1948).

Graves, Robert. *The Greek Myths*. London: Pelican Books (1955).

Graves, Robert. *New Larousse Encyclopedia of Mythology (Introduction)*. London: Hamlyn Books (1959).

Hillman, James. *The Soul's Code*. New York: Random House (1996).

Hughes-Hallet, Lucy. *Heroes: Saviours, Traitors and Supermen*. London: HarperCollins (2004).

Jung, Carl Gustav. *Four Archetypes*. London: Routledge (1972). Extract from Jung, C.G. *Collected Works Vol. 9 Part 1: The Archetypes and the Collective Unconscious*. London: Routledge (1959).

Kirk, G.S. *The Nature of Greek Myths*. London: Pelican Books (1974).

Lash, John. *The Hero: Manhood and Power*. London: Thames & Hudson (1995).

Mello, Anthony de. *The Song of the Bird*. 1st ed *Imprimatur* (1981). London: Arrow Books (1984).

Myss, Caroline. *Sacred Contracts*. New York: Harmony Books (2001).

Rank, Otto. *The Myth of the Birth of the Hero*. New York: Journal of Nervous and Mental Disease, Monograph No. 18 (1914).

Scott Peck, M. *The Road Less Travelled.* London: Random House (1978).

Schmitt, D.P. et al. *Why can't a man be more like a woman?* Journal of Personality & Social Psychology Vol 94 No 1: 168-182 (2008).

Segal, Robert. *Myth: A Very Short Introduction.* Oxford: Oxford University Press (2004).

Shah, Tahir. *In Arabian Nights.* London: TransWorld Publishers / Doubleday (2008).

Stone, Hal & Winkelman, Sidra. *Embracing Our Selves: Voice Dialogue Manual.* CA: New World Library (1989).

Vogler, Christopher. *The Writer's Journey.* USA: Michael Weise Productions (1992).

Warner, Marina. *From the Beast to the Blonde: On Fairy-Tales and their Tellers.* London: Chatto & Windus (1994).

About the Author

Jane Bailey Bain has lived and travelled extensively around the world. She studied Psychology at Oxford University and Social Anthropology at the London School of Economics. Subsequently she worked as a consultant on overseas development programmes. This involved planning and evaluating projects in terms of their practical impact on people's lives. During this time she became interested in stories and how people use them to make sense of their lives. She currently teaches in West London.

Jane was born at midnight (GMT) on Midsummer's Eve: her name is etymologically connected with the god Janus, who looks to both past and future. It was probably inevitable that she would study mythology.

BOOKS

O is a symbol of the world, of oneness and unity. In different cultures it also means the "eye," symbolizing knowledge and insight. We aim to publish books that are accessible, constructive and that challenge accepted opinion, both that of academia and the "moral majority."

Our books are available in all good English language bookstores worldwide. If you don't see the book on the shelves ask the bookstore to order it for you, quoting the ISBN number and title. Alternatively you can order online (all major online retail sites carry our titles) or contact the distributor in the relevant country, listed on the copyright page.

See our website **www.o-books.net** for a full list of over 500 titles, growing by 100 a year.

And tune in to myspiritradio.com for our book review radio show, hosted by June-Elleni Laine, where you can listen to the authors discussing their books.

MySpiritRadio